CONCILIUM

Religion in the Eighties

CONCILIUM

Concilium 161 (1/1983): Sociology of Religion

NEW RELIGIOUS MOVEMENTS

Edited by
John Coleman
and
Gregory Baum

English Language Editor
Marcus Lefébure

T. & T. CLARK LTD.
Edinburgh

THE SEABURY PRESS
New York

January 1983
T. & T. Clark Ltd., 36 George Street, Edinburgh EH2 2LQ
ISBN: 0 567 30041 2

The Seabury Press, 815 Second Avenue, New York, NY 10017
ISBN: 0 8164 2441 1

Library of Congress Catalog Card No.: 82 062754

Printed in Scotland by William Blackwood & Sons Ltd., Edinburgh

Concilium: Monthly except July and August
Subscriptions 1983: UK and Rest of the World £27·00, postage and handling included; USA and Canada, all applications for subscriptions and enquiries about *Concilium* should be addressed to The Seabury Press, 815 Second Avenue, New York, NY 10017, USA.

CONTENTS

Editorial

BECAUSE THE editors of this issue live in Toronto and Berkeley, California, our own personal exposure to representatives of new religious movements has been considerable. Representatives of Hare Krishna, The Unification Church of Rev. Moon or of Sikh, Yoga and Zen groups gravitate to the vicinities of our large universities. While the new religious movements are centred in university cities in North America and the great metropolises of Europe, they are, by no means, limited to these locales.

Various sociological studies have estimated that between 4-5 per cent of the North American young people aged 21-35 have had some exposure—even if sporadic—to new religious movements of Oriental origin.[1] Even more significant are statistics which estimate that between 35-30 per cent of this population hold favourable attitudes towards the new religions, particularly Zen, Tibetan Buddhism and Yoga.[2] Clearly, in North America the new religious movements are neither transitory nor marginal. Moreover, as the recently published census of world religions, *The World Christian Encyclopedia*, demonstrates, the new religions are to be found everywhere around the globe.[3] Presently they number some ninety-six million adherents. By the year 2,000 they will approximate in numbers to Eastern Orthodoxy. Their numbers alone warrant a serious investigation into this growing phenomenon.

The phase, 'new religious movements', serves as a mantle for an extraordinary variety of diverse groups. In general, sociologists who study the new religions join together under this rubric the three fastest growing sectors of religion in the West: neo-orthodox or neo-fundamentalist versions of Christianity and Judaism (in some cases, but not most, these are oriented to the counter-culture);[4] neo-Orientalism in Europe and the United States; various human potential movements which have been influenced by neo-Oriental ideas such as Werner Erhardt's EST and forms of trans-personal psychology.

In this issue we investigate all three kinds of groups. Christopher O Donnell and Christian Lalive D'Epinay treat of Christian neo-orthodox groups, neo-Pentecostalism in Europe and America and Pentecostalism in Chile respectively. The majority of the articles in this issue deal with neo-Orientalism (Dan O'Hanlon's report of the experience of westerners who went East to join ashrams and monasteries. Robert Ellwood's historical account of neo-Orientalism in America, Bert Hardin and Reinhart Hummel's description of Asiatic religions in Europe with a focus on the controversial Bhagwan Shree Rajneesh). This emphasis on neo-Oriental new religions is quite deliberate in order to highlight the way in which the emergence of neo-Oriental groups in the West raises anew the question of Christianity's imperative dialogue with world religions.

Although it is not customary in most studies of new religious movements to include reports of religious dialogue in Asia, this issue includes reports of Christian dialogue with Hinduism in India and Buddhism in Japan (articles by Arnulf Camps and Jan van Bragt). Ultimately, these attempts at serious dialogue between Christians and Buddhists and Christians and Hindus in Asia may give us needed clues about the direction such dialogue should take between Christianity and neo-Oriental offshoots of Hinduism and Buddhism in the West.

Missing from this issue is any historical, cultural investigation which would document, from the Asian context, what indigenous developments in the East lead to missionary movements among Asian religions. Perhaps paradigmatic would be the experience of Swami Vivekenanda in the late nineteenth century who conceived of a Hindu mission to the West precisely as a response to the challenge of Christian missions to India. As this example reminds us, we cannot fully understand the emergence of neo-Orientalism in the West unless we recall the impact of the western missionary outreach to Asia on revitalising traditional eastern forms of religion. Even the vision of the Rev. Moon is somewhat a mirror of the anti-Communism and patriotism of Presbyterian missionaries to Korea. As Jan van Bragt reminds us, neo-Oriental missions to the West bring home to us the experience, long-since available in Asia, of trans-cultural religious transplants.

Some sociologists of religion, such as Bryan Wilson, sharply distinguish between new religious movements in the Third World (Spirit Churches in Africa, the Cargo Cult in Melasia and various millennial nativistic movements) and the new religions in Europe and the North American countries.[5] Wilson argues that the new religions in Africa and Melasia are parallel to the Protestant ethic in that they represent transformative religions of modernisation and change. He relegates the new religions in Europe and the United States, on the other hand, to epiphenomenal symptoms of a further stage of the ongoing secularisation and privatisation of religion. Other sociologists of religion, such as Robert Bellah, see the new religious movements as symptoms of a major cultural transformation in western sensibilities and spirituality.[6]

As one careful student of the new religions, Steven Tipton, has put it, the new religions 'give precedence to direct experience over abstract reasoning, to "being here now" over future-oriented achievement, to harmonising with nature and others over utilising them'. With Bellah, Tipton sees the new religious movements as laboratory specimens of counter-cultural ideals. Tipton sums up the cultural conflict between these new religions and dominant western culture in these following sets of contrasts:

(1) ecstatic experience v. technical reason.
(2) holism v. analytic discrimination.
(3) acceptance v. problem solving activism.
(4) intuitive certainty v. pluralistic relativism.[7]

Anthony, Robbins and Schwartz take up the controverted issue of the cultural significance of new religious movements in the first article in this issue. In the main, they agree with the views of Bellah and Tipton rather than those of Wilson. For his part, Dan O'Hanlon cryptically ends his article in this issue by pointing to the issue of cultural conflict: 'I guess you could say that what they would like to see is not new religions, but a transformation of the United States' culture as a whole.'

In order to test Wilson's claim of a major difference between new religious movements in the Third World and those in Europe and the United States, this issue includes an essay on new religions in Africa by Clive Dillon-Malone and new religions in Latin America by Christian Lalive D'Epinay. Because *Concilium* is a theological journal, we have included two, quite different, treatments of the theological and religious significance of the new religions. Richard Bergeron, using a typological method, reduces the new religious movements to versions of neo-gnosticism, incompatible with Christianity. For his part, John Coleman attempts to suggest a quite different view of the new religions which would take its cues for the appropriate response of the Church to the new religious movements in the West from the earlier dialogue with Buddhism and Hinduism in Asia. The use of the comparative historical method, a search for 'analogous depths' in one's own religion to elements in Asiatic religions and dialogue rather than anathema, typify this suggested approach. While Bergeron focuses primarily on the ontology, soteriology and doctrines of the neo-Oriental religions, Coleman sees their fundamental challenge to the Christian

Churches in their transformative practice of meditation.

A number of sociologists of religion resist the inclusion of human potential movements as examples of 'new religions' as an improper inclusiveness. They prefer to see these various psychological movements as 'secular' rather than religious. Nevertheless, as Bert Hardin and Reinhart Hummel's article in this issue shows, there has been a great deal of contact and dialogue between eastern gurus and western trans-personal psychologists at human potential centres such as the famed Esalen Center in California. Bhagwan Shree Rajneesh exemplifies one form of this exotic marriage of eastern ideas and western techniques of psychology. Werner Erhardt's EST drawing eclectically on Zen, is yet another.[8]

Robert Ellwood in his contribution to this issue recalls for us that there have been many waves of neo-Orientalism since the latter part of the nineteenth century. What then, is *new* about neo-Orientalism? What is new is the scope, variety and numbers of adherents and diverse groups to be found in the West. At some point a critical mass accumulates where quantitative shifts have qualitative implications for a whole culture. Also new is the growing insistence on *direct experience* through meditative techniques rather than the mere imbibing of ideas from lectures and books. Finally, it seems appropriate to apply the term, 'new' to any religion whose ties to its society's recognised organised religions and culture are problematic in that the religion (1) is based on religious forms of another culture; (2) presents a radical shift or reversal of cultural trends; and (3) offers a unique combination of elements which in themselves and in isolation may be familiar.

It is true that Oriental religions undergo a 'sea change' in being translated from Asia to North America and Europe. Nevertheless, even over time, neo-Oriental religions in Europe and America diverge widely from the dominant cultural forms of religion. As 'strange' transplants they are neither more exotic nor more 'impure' than the transplants of western Christianity to Asia and Africa eighty years ago. Certainly, the new religions adapt to their new locales but in ways which show decided continuities with the ideas, techniques and world-view of the religion of origin.[9] When, however, all roots with the Asiatic tradition are lost, the danger exists of a kind of uncontrolled electicism as in Bhagwan Shree Rajneesh and other 'traditionless' gurus.

Given the enormous variety of the new religious movements, is it possible to make any valid generalisations about them? A few sociological generalisations can be ventured. First, not surprisingly, they recruit disproportionately among young people, aged 20-35.[10] Different groups appeal to different social class backgrounds. Thus, Tipton found that his Christian counter-cultural 'Jesus' group drew mainly from upwardly mobile lower and lower-middle class groups. EST recruited from upwardly mobile professional middle-class groups and *Zen* drew from a downwardly mobile upper-middle class, highly educated population. Sexually, the new religions mirror the configuration of other religious groups in the West by being disproportionately female in membership.[11]

The religious background of recruits is disproportionately Jewish, Catholic and from those of no religious background.[12] At least in North America, the new religions are more successful in recruiting the non-churched than any other group. The growing neo-Orthodox Christian groups tend to recruit mainly from re-cycled Protestant evangelicals rather than from those of no religion. Of interest is the finding of Robert Wuthnow that, contrary to expectations, the adherents of new religions do not represent the classic world-denying, world-fleeing mysticisms. Rather they exhibit social concerns and embody what Wuthnow terms, 'an inner-worldly mysticism'. This may be explained by the impact of the milieu of western activist culture upon them.[13]

There is a striking convergence among many of the studies of the new religious movements about the characteristic motives given by adherents to explain their conversion to new religions. In general what the young adherents of the new religions seem to be seeking can be summed up in the following three goals:

(1) A search for an intense *experience* of the self and the transformative sacred. Almost all commentators on the new religious movements place great stress on this theme of the search for a tangible, experimental religion.

(2) The search for a supportive community.

(3) The search for the power of personal religious experience, the authentic charisma of religious leaders and the fellowship of other devotees.[14]

It seems unlikely that these three searches are restricted to those who actually join new religious movements. Inasmuch as other members of the same age cohort as those who join new religious movements are likely also to be seeking for these three values, the new religious movements present a clear cultural challenge to the Church to find appropriate Christian embodiments of experimental religion, genuine community and authentic charisma.

JOHN COLEMAN

Notes

1. See George Gallop *Religion in America 1979-80* (Princeton Religion Research Center 1980) p. 36.

2. See Robert Wuthnow *The Consciousness Reformation* (Berkeley 1976) p. 33; for Canadian data see Frederick Bird and Bill Reimer 'Participation Rates in New Religious and Para-Religious Movements' *Journal for the Scientific of Religion* 21, no. 1 (March 1982) 1-13.

3. *The World Christian Encyclopedia* (New York 1982).

4. For a study of a counter-cultural 'Jesus sect' see Steven Tipton *Getting Saved from the Sixties* (Berkeley 1982) pp. 31-94.

5. Bryan Wilson *Contemporary Transformations of Religion* (New York 1976).

6. See *The New Religious Consciousness* eds Charles Glock and Robert Bellah (Berkeley 1976).

7. Tipton, the work cited in note 4, p. 20.

8. For an analysis of EST see Tipton, *ibid.* pp. 176-231.

9. For the adaptation of Zen to its American context, see Tipton, *ibid.* pp. 95-175.

10. See Wuthnow, the work cited in note 2, p. 154 ff and Bird and Reimer, the work cited in note 2.

11. Tipton, the work cited in note 4.

12. Data supplied by the Center for the Study of New Religious Movements, Berkeley, California.

13. Robert Wuthnow, the work cited in note 2, p. 123 ff.

14. For these characteristic motives of conversion see Glock and Bellah, the work cited in note 6; Tipton, the work cited in note 4; Harvey Cox *Turning East* (New York 1977); and Dan O'Hanlon's contribution to this issue.

Dick Anthony, Thomas Robbins and Paul Schwartz

Contemporary Religious Movements and the Secularisation Premiss

THE UNITED STATES and Western Europe are presently undergoing a period of marked spiritual ferment and innovation, which for some observers has evoked comparisons to the American 'Great Awakenings' of the eighteenth and nineteenth centuries. The key elements of the current 'awakening' appear to be: (1) a rapid growth of strident evangelical, fundamentalist and Pentecostal movements both within established churches and as new sects; (2) a parallel growth in the popularity of 'eastern' (Hindu-Buddhist-Sufi) religions; (3) a similar spread of quasi-religious 'Human Potential' movements (e.g., EST, Scientology, Arica) which combine Oriental-mystical meanings with pop psychology; (4) the emergence of several controversial authoritarian sects or 'cults', that seem to appeal especially to young persons. Several aspects of this religious ferment have become matters of considerable social concern. The most widely debated of these have to do with the complex question of civil liberties and religious freedom surrounding the tactics of 'brainwashing', allegedly used by some of these new religious groups to get and keep converts; and the equally controversial practice of 'deprogramming' techniques by various anti-cult groups to 'free' these converts. Another widely discussed issue has to do with social attitudes and actions of members of these new religious movements. Does adherence to these new religious movements necessarily breed conservative political views? Or, does it lead to an egoistic stance that produces withdrawal from socio-political concerns? A more fundamental issue arises because the current apparent upsurge in religious activity seems to represent a dramatic reversal of a long-term trend towards a diminution of the importance of religions, or at least of theistic and supernaturalistic religions, in our society. For over one hundred years, it has been assumed within the main intellectual currents of our society that religion would continuously—and inevitably—lose influence as the result of the process of modernisation (a 'secularisation' theme). Does the current 'awakenings' contradict that assumption?

These themes were presented above in the reverse of the order in which they will be discussed in this article. We will argue that the issues embodied in controversies over 'narcissism', religious authoritarianism and brainwashing are in part derivative from the broader issues of secularisation and the compatibility of religion and modernity.

In general, the secularisation premiss has held that religion—or at least the theistic and supernaturalistic forms of religion—will inevitably lose influence within modern

1

society. Numerous arguments have been put forth which interpret religion as an outmoded way of conceptualising psychological, sociological and economic truths about man and society. Psychoanalytic views interpret religion as a system of rationalisations and psychological defences. Marxian analyses view religion as a form of 'false consciousness' that masks class interests and reflects alienation. The more recent Skinnerian presentation views religion as a perpetuation of a false image of man that mistakenly emphasises free will and obscures the deterministic nature of actual human decision-making. From the standpoint of all of these perspectives, *any 'revival' or reemergence of religions with supernaturalistic orientations would be, necessarily, regressive*. These perspectives are very widely shared, not only among social scientists but also among 'lay' citizens. They yield an essentially secular outlook, which views religion—or at least emotionally fervent and life-pervading religions—as inherently pathological and repressive in the context of today's world.

Until recently, the evidence regarding religious attitudes and behaviour would seem to support the secularisation thesis for both Western Europe and the United States. In Western Europe, Church membership has declined throughout the twentieth century. In the United States, membership in mainline Protestant churches has remained relatively constant for the past century except for a brief upswing in the 1950s followed by a decline in the 1960s. But during that period there has been a shift in the content of beliefs within those mainline Protestant denominations. Specifically, there has been a decline in belief in the supernaturalistic motifs of those religions which have been interpreted as having only 'symbolic' meaning. There has also been an increase in the importance of beliefs related to the social and ethical dimensions of Christianity. These developments are compatible with the secularisation perspectives described above, which imply some mode of rational humanism as the best hope for human progress.

Recent trends challenge the secularisation perspective. Liberal mainstream religion has not continued to grow during the late 1960s and 1970s. On the other hand, in the United States there has been rapid growth in the conservative and fundamentalist Protestant churches while the liberal denominations have either declined or remained static.[1] Even within liberal denominations and within Catholicism there are marked evangelical tendencies and Pentecostal or 'charismatic' movements. The most dynamic parts of Judaism currently seem to be the neo-Orthodox revival and the growth of quasi-sectarian groups such as the Hassidim.

There is considerable heterogeneity among the new religious movements. What all these movements have in common is an emphasis on emotional fervour and/or inner spiritual 'experience'. That is, they all include the premiss that *one comes by authentic values by means of intense experiences rather than by means of rational thought and analysis*. Thus, the conspicuous trends in contemporary religion in America—the evangelical upsurge, orientalism, and the proliferation of quasi-religious therapeutic groups—seem to embody a rejection of the rational humanism towards which liberal religion seemed to have been evolving.[2]

We are dealing with a phenomenon of major scope and some persistence. It bears on the secularisation thesis and especially on the common assumption that supernaturalism is outmoded and dying. The relative growth of evangelical churches seems to foreshadow the increasing influence of conservative religious attitudes. Equally incongruent from the standpoint of the secularisation perspective is the rise of arational mystical orientations embodied in guru and human potential groups. These movements recruit their clientele largely from affluent, urbanised, and highly educated segments of the population.[3] These are the same groups who have formerly been in the vanguard of trends towards rational secular humanism.

The main response of adherents of the secularisation perspective to the present ferment, though, has been to argue that today's proliferating religious sects and quasi-religious therapies represent either *trivial* or *pathological* phenomena, which lack the creative, community-building, culture-forming force associated with the religions of prior historical epochs. Three distinct arguments can be discerned: (1) the 'trivialisation thesis' recently articulated by Bryan Wilson; (2) the 'narcissism' thesis, most often applied to guru-meditation-therapy movements; and (3) the charge that ruthless cult leaders are winning adherents through 'brainwashing'.

Bryan Wilson, an eminent sociologist of religion, sees the current proliferation of exotic spiritual forms 'as a confirmation of the process of secularisation'. The new movements 'indicate the degree to which religion has become inconsequential for modern society'.[4] Today's 'cults' reduce religion to an exotic consumer item. Identity seekers 'shop' for exotic and provocatively packaged spiritual mystiques in a growing 'spiritual supermarket'. Yet their choice of religious consumption has 'no real consequences for other social institutions, for political power structures, for technological constraints and controls'.[5]

Wilson contrasts today's profusion of 'cults' with prior episodes of spiritual ferment and awakening such as the Methodist revival in early nineteenth-century England. In the earlier 'awakenings', social control was still grounded in personal and group relations, so that it was possible for the spread of new spiritual orientations to transform the social structure, the economy, and the culture. In modern society, however, the 'privatisation' of religion has already isolated religious values from other aspects of life. The dominant bureaucratic structures are indifferent to religious orientation. Whether one is a 'born-again Christian' or does Transcendental Meditation in the evenings will not have a significant effect on one's role performance in a bureaucracy. Thus, today's 'cults' and religio-therapies *epitomise the modern reduction of religion to an exotic consumer item and a colourful adornment of personal style.*

In effect, Wilson is arguing that today's 'cults' are not really 'religions' in the sociological sense in which early modern religions (e.g., eighteenth-century Methodism) were. They are not *prophetic* religions with a potential for creatively transforming the socio-cultural order. They are marginal phenomena, in spite of their apparent vitality.

Wilson's view is close to that of Christopher Lasch, who argues that today's human-potential and meditation groups are *not true religions* because they lack a Utopian element, which he considers essential to authentic religions.[6] Contemporary religio-therapeutic mystiques adjust their clients to the *status quo*, but they do so without offering a vision of an alternative 'better world' either here or in the hereafter. For Lasch, the proliferating mystical and therapeutic movements are direct reflections of a 'narcissism' that is widespread in contemporary America.

'Narcissism' has become a vague, overused term. Lasch and others have used the term 'narcissism' to characterise both the present popularisation of eastern mysticism and the rapid growth of quasi-mystical psychotherapeutic movements. But other writers have applied the term 'narcissism' more broadly to the whole range of contemporary spiritual tendencies, including the evangelical upsurge and the growth of groups such as The Unification Church, all of which allegedly reflect an intense self-fixation.[7] At least three meanings of the term 'narcissism' can be distinguished:

(a) Narcissism as a force for social apathy and passivity

Sociologist Edwin Schur's book on the Human Potential Movement is entitled *The Awareness Trap: Self-Absorption Instead of Social Change.*[8] He argues that today's putative self-actualisers are totally pre-occupied with concerns about inner 'consciousness' to the exclusion of concerns for the welfare of others and for social change. Another writer has seen the growing mystical passivity as a threat to democracy and has envisioned a future involving 'some IBM-type of economic and political control over a mystified population escaping into occultism'.[9]

(b) Narcissism as a force for socio-political conservatism

Peter Marin[10] and others have argued that certain elements of today's quasi-mystical therapeutic perspectives have conservative effects. It has been noted that some persons actually believe that the Bengalis are starving *because* their consciousness had not developed sufficiently or *because* it is their *Karma* to starve. Popular quasi-mystical orientations often entail a 'harmonial' theme emphasising the natural harmony or rhythm of the universe. One must get in tune with this natural rhythm, rather than seek in vain to control the spontaneous process of life. This dogma may imply that goal-oriented human intervention in the 'natural rhythm' of socio-economic processes is futile. This posture 'fits' the alleged shift in American political attitudes towards the right, as exemplified by the growing antipathy towards government spending and taxation. Such an argument is also congruent with the results of several surveys on values in the 1970s, which report a restriction of social empathy, and a decline in the expectation that social problems can be resolved through collective action.[11]

(c) Narcissism as a psychopathological condition

Lasch and others argue that mystical religious orientations are rationalisations for *obsessive self-fixation* which in turn points to an inability to sustain long-term commitments and relationships of any sort. It is asserted that this pattern reflects 'permissive' child-rearing practices which hinder the development of strong parental identifications. Pathological 'narcissism' is culturally legitimated by ideological celebration of the 'self'.

Lasch, Schur, and others have interpreted the growth of new religions and therapies as representing an *amplification* of narcissistic themes already pervasive within American culture. An alternative analysis might view these movements as *reactions against* narcissistic and privatistic trends. This argument is implicit in a recent paper by Benton Johnson, who argues that the decline of American 'civil religion' involves an erosion of widely shared religious and ideological beliefs that 'have linked together private and public sectors'.[12] The result has been to intensify the traditional 'protestant' disjuncture between the 'cure of souls' and the concern for bettering society. The explosion of privatised mystical and therapeutic movements reflects this disjuncture. In Johnson's view the label of 'narcissism' is more applicable to new *therapies* such as EST or Scientology than to new *religions* such as The Unification Church, Hare Krishna, or Meher Baba, which mitigate the consequences of narcissism by encouraging moral constraints, self-discipline, and social altruism. Yet these groups have little potential for decisively resolving the widening disjuncture between self-oriented and socially-oriented values.

Few of the critics of 'narcissism' in new religions and therapies have actually conducted research on the new movements. Nor do they seem familiar with other research on this topic. Their conclusions seem largely determined by an assumption that mystical religion is intrinsically irresponsible in modern society. What little research has been done on these issues suggests different conclusions. Nordquist found a high level of 'social compassion' among members of the Ananda Yoga community in California.[13] The San Francisco Bay Area Survey found positive correlations between mystical orientations and political activism, liberalism, and approval of social experimentation on the other.[14] Robert Wuthnow has recently challenged some of the basic assumptions underlying the assumed negative relationship between mystical 'passivity' and political activism.[15] Wuthnow argues that the epistemology of mysticism, which involves a direct intuitive apprehension of truth, detaches mystics from dominant institutionalised perspectives and can lead to a critical and reformist antinomianism.

By and large, there has been too little systematic research on new religions and therapies to permit an evaluation of the arguments put forth in the 'narcissism' literature. At present, we know very little about the social consequences of recent spiritual trends. It is likely that *different groups and movements will have different social consequences*.[16] This view is congruent with Johnson's position and with some recent typologising of new religious groups.

The majority of 'new religions' are actually relatively accommodative towards dominant social institutions. The devotee often pursues his career during the week and goes to the ashram, monastery, or retreat on the weekend or during the summer. There has emerged a subset of authoritarian communal groups, however, which have aroused fierce hostility. Such 'extreme cults' are accused of 'brainwashing' their converts and 'breaking up families'. An 'anti-cult' movement has emerged, which views cult leaders such as Reverend Sun Myung Moon as demonic figures who seek to enslave young persons through techniques of 'mind control' that produce a kind of demonic possession.

The anti-cult movement has supported the tactics of *deprogramming*, which involves intensive counter-indoctrination, usually accompanied by physical confinement. Deprogrammers argue that groups such as The Unification Church or Hare Krishnas are really 'pseudo-religions' whose members are manipulated into 'pseudo-conversions' by cult leaders. Deprogramming is thus promoted as a liberating technique which emancipates individuals from mental enslavement and restores them to autonomy.

Implicit in the perspective which supports deprogramming is the application of the *medical model* to religious commitments. An extreme version of this application is the assertion by Dr Eli Shapiro, MD, that young persons joining religious cults develop a real disease, 'destructive cultism' which can be scientifically diagnosed but requires innovative treatment (deprogramming).[17] A number of psychologists and mental health professionals have embraced the notion that indoctrination in a 'cult' produces a form of regressive psychopathology and is, moreover, a 'coercive' experience which destroys free will.

It appears to be widely assumed that *no one would ever voluntarily surrender intellectual freedom and flexibility*; hence those who submit to sectarian regimentation must have been coercively persuaded to do so. But people have been voluntarily joining totalistic movements for centuries, and much of the literature on Christianity in its first century of existence depicts the early Christians in totalistic and authoritarian terms.[18] Life-pervading religious commitments are deviant in modern America and are thus assumed to be pathological and characterised by inauthentic, unmotivated participation.

Recent research on contemporary religious movements suggests that the 'coercive' quality of recruitment and indoctrination is somewhat limited. Very few individuals who are approached by cultist recruiters or who attend an initial indoctrination session subsequently participate further. The intensely stigmatised Unification Church of Reverend Sun Myung Moon actually has a *substantial voluntary defection rate*—disaffected participants continually walk away, 'coercion' and 'mind control' notwithstanding.[19]

Recently a widely read book, *Snapping: America's Epidemic of Sudden Personality Change*,[20] seems to have synthesised elements of the brainwashing and narcissism themes. The argument employs a model of the proper functioning of the mind in which thoughts and information must be processed in a manner analogous to the process by which scientists evaluate data. The authors seem to interpret any intense involvement in very generalised symbolic realities which cannot be verified by rational-empirical criteria but which have empirical consequences for controlling behaviour as evidence for the pathological syndrome of 'snapping'.

A person who has 'snapped' has regressed to a sort of mechanical subhuman state; he or she is operating somewhat as an automaton without critically evaluating the environment. 'Snapping' is associated by the authors with mystical cults, human potential groups and evangelical-Pentecostal movements. People heavily involved in these groups are said to be victims of 'information disease'. Authoritarian and puritanical sects which superficially seem to have repudiated pervasive hedonism and narcissism have in fact extrapolated mindless hedonism by creating homogeneous enclaves in which the uncritical acceptance of authoritarian leadership is exchanged for immediate gratification of a sensual or emotional nature. But the authors also see a similar if less extreme pattern in the mainstream culture where victims of media manipulation and pathological consumerism surrender their critical faculties to parasitic corporate leaders whose products provide them with immediate emotional gratifications.

The theory of *Snapping* is really untestable. The authors' discussion of the effect of cult rituals in blocking information transmission in the nervous system is speculative. Although the authors discuss 'the snapping moment' and generally depict the onset of information disease as a sudden discontinuous event, they also speak of 'snapping in slow motion', and assert that a process of evolutionary conversion would not disprove their theory. It thus seems warranted to view the theory as a derivation from the premiss that strong and comprehensive involvements with generalised symbolic realities is pathological and regressive.

The current religious ferment in America is substantial and somewhat persistent. Critical commentary has ranged from treatment of these movements as representing a trivialisation of religion in modern America; to concern for assumed undesirable effects of such religions on social attitudes; to treatment of them as psychopathology. Much of this negative commentary stems from an underlying premiss about the inevitable secularisation of modern society. A century of increasing secularisation has led to the development of a broadly shared norm to the effect that 'real' or legitimate or 'healthy' religion should emphasise rational/humanistic/social concerns and de-emphasise intuitive/emotional and supernatural themes as much as possible. The new religious movements do not fit this picture; hence they are viewed as either not real religions, and/or as unhealthy conditions for their adherents, the society, or both.

Controversies over today's alternative religions thus entail conflicts between *conflicting models of humanity*. We have argued that the above critiques of the new religions as either socially regressive or psychopathological are dependent upon one version or another of the secularisation hypothesis as an often unstated presupposition. In our view, interpretations of involvement in these groups as the effect of 'brainwashing' or some pathological syndrome can only be considered reasonable if one grants unqualified validity to a basic tenet of the secularisation hypothesis: namely, that widespread adoption of the worldview of scientific humanism is a historical necessity.

In conclusion, we propose an alternative perspective for the interpretation of today's new religions. Our view is grounded in a Weberian analysis of the process of *rationalisation* in the social world and of the different types of rationalism developing in western culture. We contest the assumption that the domination of the 'scientific' worldview and its attendant images of the human is uniquely legitimate and, moreover, historically necessary.

We find Max Weber's analysis salient to the issues at hand because of its focus on the process of rationalisation. In delimiting the development of modern rationalism, he meant to refer to it *as only one of several possible types of rationalism* that together permeate the social world. In his elaboration of the Protestant Ethic hypothesis, Weber makes clear the existence of two other spheres open to the effects of rationalisation at the birth of the modern era. Wolfgang Schluchter [21] delineates these possible types as 'ethico-metaphysical rationalism' and 'practical rationalism'; both stand alongside the more familiar scientific-technical rationalism.

Indeed, Weber's point in *The Protestant Ethic and the Spirit of Capitalism* was to indicate how the schism between western *scientific-technical* and *ethico-metaphysical* rationalism enabled the formation in the West of the particular type of *practical* rationalism. This disjunction legitimates the creation of social forms and individual behaviours amenable to the development and expansion of entrepreneurial capitalism in Northern Europe and the United States.

Weber not only indicated the significance of this decisive disjunction of previously unified forms of rationalism; he demonstrated as well how this particular expression of technical rationalism tended to reduce the significance of a now-transcendent ethical-metaphysical rationalism in modern society. The three types of rationalism outlined by Weber not only emerged as distinct; once distinct, they tended to develop independently of one another, each following its own inner logic and reason.

This sketch of Weber's analysis puts in context the contemporary problematic raised by advocates of the secularisation hypothesis. The analysis of religion phenomena according to the canons of positive science erected on the foundations of modern scientific rationalism has achieved so dominant a position in contemporary thought that it has reduced to trivial or fanatic the claims of *any* ethical rationalism, the latter forever banished to the inconsequential realm of the other-worldly.

We wish to suggest an alternative interpretation of contemporary religious phenomena. The emergence of new religions can be interpreted as the effect of a widespread perception in certain western societies of the inadequacy of scientific-technical rationalism alone to orient contemporary social life. This perception, it can be argued, lies behind what emerged as political radicalism in the 1960s and now continues in some of the new movements which can thus be viewed as the surviving remnants of the Sixties counterculture in modern societies.

The assumption underlying normative secularisaion theory that the exclusive dominance of scientific rationalism is both necessary and inevitable for modern culture is debatable. The positions examined above all seem to assume that participation in novel religious movements necessarily imparts to believers an unhealthy perspective on the role of reason in personal and group life. However, given the apparent dominance of technical rationality in western culture—with its circumscription of reason itself—and the alienating effects of this dominance for both individuals and society, the appeal of the new religious groups to something 'other' might be considered sane and prophetic. One effect of the reduction of 'reason' to 'scientific-technical' reason is to occlude the role of values in social life. This leaves the whole realm of expressive behaviour in effect *unstructured by values*. This sphere is given over to irrational determination by a mindless consumerism. The new religions, in their appeal to *transrational imagery and symbol*, at least open the possibility of a reintegration of values and practical rationalities.[22] Whether or not specific groups achieve this goal is of course subject to question.

In our view, more research is needed to allow discrimination between movements on the basis of the ethical possibilities inherent in their rituals, beliefs, and images of the human. Not all the 'new religions' offer valuable alternatives to the technocratic society. But neither does the humanist religion of the cultural mainstream. Investigation should focus on the elements within these religious systems which facilitate a re-vitalisation of religion. Too general an orientation—like that of the critiques noted above, which rest at bottom on a normative option for the secularisation thesis—will obscure rather than enlighten present alternatives.

Notes

1. See D. Kelley *Why the Conservative Churches are Growing* (New York 1972).
2. Evidence from surveys over the past decade indicates that both mystical and evangelical movements are neither transitory nor marginal phenomena. See for example W. Roof and C. Hadaway 'Shifts in Religious Preference in the Mid-seventies' *Journal for the Scientific Study of Religion* 16 (1977) 317-321; and Andrew Greeley *Sociology of the Paranormal: A Reconnaissance* (Beverly Hills).
3. R. Wuthnow *Experimentation in American Religion* (Berkeley).
4. B. Wilson *Contemporary Transformations of Religion* (Oxford 1976) p. 96.
5. B. Wilson *ibid.* p. 96.
6. C. Lasch *The Culture of Narcissism* (New York 1979).
7. See, for example, J. Fichter 'The Trend to Spiritual Narcissism' *Commonweal* 105 (1978) 169-172.
8. E. Schur *The Awareness Trap* (New York 1976).
9. H. Drietzel 'On the Political Meaning of Culture' in *Beyond the Crisis* ed. N. Birnbaum (New York 1977) pp. 83-132.
10. P. Marin 'The New Narcissism: The Trouble with the Human Potential Movement' *Harpers* 251, 45-56.
11. D. Yankelovich 'New Rules in American Life' *Psychology Today* (April 1981) 76-78.
12. B. Johnson 'A Sociological Perspective on the New Religions' in *In Gods We Trust* ed. T. Robbins and D. Anthony (New Brunswick 1981) 51-66.
13. T. Nordquist *Anada Cooperative Village* (Uppsala 1978).
14. Wuthnow, the work cited in note 3.
15. R. Wuthnow 'Political Aspects of the Quietistic Revival' in T. Robbins and D. Anthony, the work cited in note 12, 229-242.
16. See T. Robbins, D. Anthony and J. Richardson 'Theory and Research on Today's "New Religions"' *Sociological Analysis* 39, 95-122.
17. E. Shapiro 'Destructive Cultism' *American Family Physician* 15, 80-83.
18. One writer has compared early Christianity with Communism: E. Dodds *Pagan and Christian in An Age of Anxiety* (New York 1963) pp. 133-134.
19. See T. Robbins and D. Anthony 'Deprogramming, Brainwashing and the Medicalization of Deviant Religious Groups' *Social Problems* 29 (In press); and D. Anthony, J. Needleman and T. Robbins *Conversion, Coercion and Commitment in New Religions Movements* (New York) In press.
20. F. Conway and J. Siegelman *Snapping* (New York 1978).
21. W. Schluchter 'The Paradox of Rationalisation' in G. Roth and W. Schluchter *Max Weber's Vision of History* (Berkeley 1979).
22. Arguably transrational or transpersonal phenomena are frequently interpreted as pre-rational or pre-personal, see K. Wilber 'The Pre/Trans Fallacy' *Re-Vision* 3 (1980) 51-72.

John Coleman

The Religious Significance of New Religious Movements

IT IS artificial and arbitrary to separate the two categories of the cultural and the religious significance of new religious movements. As Paul Tillich reminds us in his famous *dictum*, 'religion is the substance of culture and culture is the form of religion'. Hence, the questions which Anthony, Robbins and Schwartz raise in their article in this issue are important for determining an informed response to the religious significance of the new religious movements. Are they harbingers of a new reformation of religious consciousness akin to the rise of the Protestant ethic in the sixteenth century? Are they basically epiphenomena of a wider secularisation and privatisation of religion, following a market model of alternative consumer religions?[1]

The new religious movements represent, world-wide, a challenge to the mainline Christian denominations. They are growing apace. Currently, they comprise 2·2 per cent of the world population, some ninety-six million. They presently outnumber Judaism and by the year 2000 will approximate to the numbers of Eastern Orthodoxy.[2] Various sociological studies indicate that the new religious in Europe and North America are more successful than mainline churches in recruiting young members and, especially, in gaining adherents among those whose background is un-churched.[3]

As the editorial introduction of this issue makes clear, it is necessary to distinguish between various types and forms of new religious movements. Eclectic gurus such as James Jones and Bhagwan Shree Rajneesh should not be equated with western importations of authentic Oriental forms of religion such as Zen, Buddhism, Sufism and Yoga. The focus of this article will be on the religious challenge to the mainline Christian denominations by *authentic* forms of neo-Orientalism. It will also suggest an appropriate response from the churches. In addressing the challenge of the explosive emergence of new religions to mainline Christianity I will not, naïvely, assume that if Christianity were to adopt its own forms of the ashram, Zen Centre or guru it would successfully compete for western adherents who now join neo-Oriental religions. There is absolutely no sociological evidence to suggest this is an inevitable possibility. The fundamental religious challenge to Christianity is to recover elements of its own authentic—if lost—tradition whether or not this retrieval entails any greater success in recruiting new young adherents.

The religious challenge of neo-Orientalism to mainline Christianity strikes me as twofold. First, a flourishing neo-Orientalism (even if only a minority segment of *circa*

9

1-2 per cent of the population) in the West confronts Europe and North America directly with the imperative dialogue between Christianity and the world religions. No longer can this remain the affair of the Christian minorities in Japan, Sri Lanka and India. Jan van Bragt captures this first challenge in his article about the dialogue between Buddhism and Christianity in Japan in this issue in the summary judgment: 'In so far as they really contribute to that awareness in Christianity and, hence, to involving the universal Church in the dialogue with other religions, these movements must be counted a blessing.' Many students of religion see this dialogue between the world religions as the next essential step in human consciousness, calling for the creation of what Wilfred Cantwell Smith has referred to as 'a world theology'.[4] Unfortunately, up to this point, none of the mainline Christian denominations in the West have yet mounted a comprehensive and coherent response to the activities of the new cults and religious movements.[5]

The second religious challenge comes more from the neo-Oriental religions which include monastic, guru or esoteric traditions than from 'bhakti' religions such as Meher Baba which are mainly devotional in form. One of the most astute and well-informed students of new religious movements in North America and Europe, Jacob Needleman, poses this second challenge strongly in a recent book, *Lost Christianity*.[6] The title of Needleman's book suggests his thesis that elements of authentic Christianity have been lost. Needleman distinguishes, for his purposes, between Christianity as a world organisation and Christianity as an inner spiritual path. In focusing on the latter, he raises questions about the power of Christianity as 'a way', with transformative capabilities, distinctive practices and a developed, subtle and supple esoteric tradition which will enable initiates to discover an intimate knowledge of self, world, the other and God. As an inner path of transformative power, Christianity should entail: (*a*) a distinctive set of practices; (*b*) forms of intimate knowledge; (*c*) *levels* of initiation; and (*d*) an esoteric tradition.

Following the lead of St Paul, Clement of Alexandria and Origen, Needleman proposes a form of Christian *gnosis* which he sharply distinguishes from classical pagan gnosticism. In particular, Christian *gnosis* would not focus on self-awareness in isolation but on the self in the new perspective of its transformative life *in* Christ. Moreover, Christian *gnosis* would locate salvation not in knowledge but in the faith-response to the initiatory grace of God in Christ. Again, Christian *gnosis* would reject any notion that salvation is restricted to a small élite cognitive minority. It would also eschew the absolute ontological dualism inherent in pagan gnostic systems. Nevertheless, Christian faith does make claims to be a transformative practice and *gnosis*.

Needleman set out in search for 'the Christianity that works, that actually produces real change in human nature, real transformation'.[7] His complaint is lodged against the pervasive cultural forms of western Christianity. 'Religion was only a matter of words, exhortations and philosophy rather than a matter of *practical guidance* for experiencing *directly* the truth of the teachings.'[8] For the latter, a practice leading to a distinctive experience and intimate knowledge of self, self-and-God, self-and-world-under-God, and of God are necessary.

An authentic practice of Christianity as transformative religion entails multiple practical techniques of nurturing sensitivity to self-delusion and ego compulsions, finding ways to remove the impediments of ego to union with God and, more positively, methods to help mindfulness and attention so that 'in all conditions and at every moment we experience in ourselves *both* the eternal presence and the fallen ego'.[9] As this last citation makes clear, Needleman does not espouse a monism.

Needleman's criticism of Christian practice is that it fails to achieve these goals. He sees Christianity as speaking the highest language of union with God without providing the necessary means to dispose towards it. He uses terminology which might suggest the traditional triad of a purgative, illuminative and unitive way. But where are these ways supplely embodied in vigorous schools of practice in prayer? Have they become elements of discourse from the past which lack practitioners who can lead initiates along the path appropriate to their unique temperaments and stage of development?

To address this issue, Needleman introduces the concept of 'intermediate Christianity'. He argues that there are and must be *levels* of Christian experience and practice (which are not necessarily tied to levels of being graced). A first level looks to the initial struggle 'to awaken' and a second level deals with the movement to attain or predispose to the attainment of union with God. In Needleman's view, the precondition for transformative consciousness of God is the achievement of a 'unified self or soul', intermediate between ego and God. After the struggle (is it ever really over?) to overcome the delusions and compulsions of ego, one learns to become more centred, attentive, contemplative. A unified self or 'soul' is necessary if mystical union with God is to bear fruit. Despite several interviews with Christian spiritual directors and frequent visits to monasteries, Needleman did not find the embodiments of the graduated levels of Christian practice he sought to parallel the sophisticated spiritual psychologies and methods of meditation he found in several of the neo-Oriental groups he studied.

'One will have to speak of such things as freedom of choice, clear intelligence and goodness of will not as given characteristics of our being but as themselves results of inner discipline.'[10] An appropriate humanness capable of perceiving and responding to God's initiative towards union is not a product of sheer nature or the givenness of existence. It is, itself, the achievement of a practice of attention. It is this practice which Needleman sees as lost to Christianity.

The usefulness of esoteric traditions is that they provide flexible and subtle ways of focusing on energy within oneself, varying energies of dispersal and dissipation in ego, energies of attention and mindfulness in the centred, unified self and the transformative energies of undergoing the divine action. 'Not even God can help a person who has no attention.'[11] The phrase, esoteric tradition, conjures up for many westerners the dangers of élitism and gnosticism. But only an esoteric tradition is supple enough to apply ideas and methods to the appropriate level of development of each initiate and adept or to tailor practices to the characteristic virtues and vices of a given initiate.

Esoteric traditions seek to avoid being misunderstood in ways which might suggest that the consciousness and experience of union with God is the same for the person who has not yet entered a path of struggle against the delusions and compulsions of ego, the person who is trying to achieve a centred self and the person who already experiences union with God. It is Needleman's contention that 'the lost element in Christianity is the specific methods and ideas which can, first, show us the sub-human level at which we actually exist and, second, lead us towards the level at which the teachings of Christ can be followed *in fact* rather than *in imagination*.[12]

Needleman realises that the challenge of the new religions to Christianity is not simply a call to revive the mystic *texts* of the spiritual tradition of the West. More than texts, living spiritual guides and an embodied practice attentive to varying levels of Christian initiation into the life of God will be needed. Moreover, he carefully distinguishes between the methods and practice of neo-Orientalism as spiritual paths and the explicit (often monist) ontologies of their doctrines. These contentions, however, fly in the face of a widespread western antipathy to any idea of hierarchy, levels of consciousness or esoteric traditions.[13] Concern for publicness, universalisability and egalitarianism blind western thought to *any* validity in esoteric traditions.

A philosopher, Thomas Kasulis, demonstrates the close connection between 'intimate knowledge' and esotericism in an as yet unpublished paper, 'Intimacy as Heuristic Theme in Understanding Japanese Religion'. Relying on Japanese Buddhist texts, Kasulis develops his core concept of 'intimate knowledge' which he contrasts with ordinary discursive explanatory knowledge (direct assimilation v. explanation). Kasulis contrasts these two ways of knowing:

(a) Intimate knowledge is personal rather than public. Discursive knowledge, on the contrary, is more public and universalisable than personal.

(b) Intimate knowledge involves a different mode of self-relation from discursive knowledge. In intimate knowledge the self is perceived under the rubric of participatory belonging—in relation—rather than in the ordinary distancing mode of self v. object of discursive knowledge. Intimate knowledge is profoundly *participative* knowledge.

(c) In intimate knowledge, knowing and feeling are combined to create a unitary mood. Understanding occurs through the medium of an experience of the participative move rather than through experimental 'controlling' of the object or data of understanding.

(d) Intimate knowledge includes a dimension of physicality. It is practical and embodied as much as a theoretical knowledge. As with other practical, embodied knowledge such as skills, e.g., skiing or chess, only adepts can fully understand the finer points of practice. Non-initiates or non-adepts in these skills will not understand—or, worse still, actually misunderstand—the discourse of adepts.

Kasulis notes that the Japanese character for intimacy, in its root, *mitsu*, combines several meanings. This linguistic root conjures up both the ideas of intimacy and closeness and also secrecy, privacy, the non-public. Kasulis relates the two concepts of intimacy and esotericism in Japanese tradition. Two citations from his work are illustrative of this point. 'Intimate knowledge does not proceed in a step-by-step discursive manner. For this reason it cannot be taught or outlined in the way most other forms of knowledge can be. One acquires an intimate knowledge *through a disciplined apprenticeship with a master*. Furthermore, one learns it through a practical as well as intellectual activity.'[14] Again, 'Intimate knowledge is non-discursive, cannot be taught intellectually and is the result of *a disciplined psychophysical* training method'.[15]

My contention is that the basic challenge of the new religious movements to Christianity, especially those of neo-Oriental esoteric traditions, is rooted in this relation between a properly 'intimate' experiential knowledge of self, self-and-God and God and the indispensable esoteric traditions of initiation and practice which yield the experience of genuine human transformation. The young westerners Dan O'Hanlon interviewed in the research reported in this issue all felt that a genuine *experiential* practical knowledge of a way of transformation was lacking in their contact with western Christianity. Western Christianity has, perhaps rightly, been suspicious of esoteric traditions. Nevertheless, they have flourished throughout Christian history not just in books but in living schools of discipleship and initiation. Whatever the difficulties involved in esoteric traditions (e.g., élitism, the possibility of manipulation and fraud, the problem of discerning the true from the false guru), some version of esoteric tradition has evolved in almost all of the world religions. Esotericism remains a strong element in Oriental religions.

Some form of esotericism seems to meet permanent religious, even Christian needs. In losing any sense for esotericism and *levels* of Christian practice (with methods appropriate to these distinctive levels) western Christianity may have also lost the ability to help people to attain a supple and sophisticated *intimate* knowledge of both self and God. In my view, the fundamental religious challenge of the new religious movements to mainline Christianity would lead us to address again the relation between esoteric tradition, 'intimate' knowledge of self and God and a Christianity that 'works' (that actually helps people experience *directly* the transformative power of Christianity as a way to centredness and union). Not every esotericism involves gnosticism, élitism or pretentions to salvation by *gnosis*. In losing a sense of a developed esotericism and levels of Christian initiation, western Christianity may have eventuated in a 'flat' undifferentiated egalitarianism which simultaneously promises a full union with God without providing appropriate methods for the various stages of spiritual development. It lacks attention to paths and methods of religious consciousness coordinated to these stages.

THE RESPONSE OF THE CHURCHES TO THE CHALLENGE OF THE NEW RELIGIONS

As noted earlier, the mainline churches have, as yet, not mounted a comprehensive analysis and response to the new religions. In the United States, it has been mainly fundamentalist evangelical groups which have forged a coherent response and strategy for dealing with cults and the new religious movements. I want, in this section of the article, to review critically two proposed responses to the new religious movements and, then, to suggest a third, perhaps more appropriate, response of the churches.

The first proposal is one with which I am familiar. In my home city, a group called 'The Berkeley Christian Coalition', a largely fundamentalist group of evangelical churches, has targeted university students in Berkeley and members of the drug and counter-culture for special efforts of evangelisation. The Berkeley Christian Coalition sponsors a 'Spiritual Counterfeits Project' which alerts young people to the dangers of various cults operating in the San Francisco area. It has, for example, successfully challenged, in the courts, the introduction of *Transcendental Meditation* into the California public school system. They argued, in legal brief, that Transcendental Meditation is inextricably rooted in Hindu religious cosmology. Its compulsory introduction into the schools represents, therefore, a violation of the American constitutional practice of separation of Church and State.

The pamphlets and other literature of 'The Spiritual Counterfeits Project' stress that its aim is to provide a rebuttal and rejoinder to new religious movements. 'The Spiritual Counterfeits Project' views all cults as false, evil, due to the work of the Antichrist. Its avowed goal is 'to equip Christians to understand the psychology, the philosophy and spiritual dimensions of the contemporary explosion and, thereby, to demystify the mystical'.

I have three major difficulties with adopting this basically polemical approach of 'The Spiritual Counterfeits Project'. First, it represents a characteristically 'fundamentalist' animus against any form of mysticism. But mysticism is also a genuine Christian reality. Moreover, it will not do to try to lump together, as they do, all 'cults' as if Rev. Moon's *Unification Church* or *Hare Krishna* are of one piece with disciplined traditions from world religions which have been transplanted to the West from Tibet, India or Japan. Second, the evangelical fundamentalist response is unable to assert that salvation can and does occur outside of Christianity. Those who see the Christian God as also active in other world religions cannot facilely assume that *all non-Christian* forms of religion are *ipso facto* counterfeits! Third, 'The Spiritual Counterfeits Project' uses a polemical apologetics as the appropriate way to approach (perhaps, better said, *reproach*!) those who have chosen to join non-Christian movements. In an era of dialogue among the world religions this stance seems *a priori* inappropriate.

My basic sympathy with the stance of 'The Spiritual Counterfeits Project'—in the face of widespread spiritual illiteracy in the West and the attraction of authoritarian or destructive cults to many youth in North America and Europe—is contained in the question implied by the title of the group. Clearly, we need as a Christian Church to find some way to sort out 'spiritual counterfeits' from more authentic forms of neo-Orientalism, to be on our guard to warn impressionable youth against such self-destructive systems as that represented by the Reverend James Jones of Jonestown or the questionable practices of some extraordinarily 'eclectic' gurus such as Bhagwan Shree Rajneesh. Since Buddhism, Hinduism and Islam have long histories of facing the issue of 'spiritual counterfeits' v. 'authentic expressions of the tradition', using their own internal criteria, the criteria we choose to adjudicate between various movements might be drawn from the great world traditions themselves. Each has its own set of criteria based on canonical scriptures, traditional lineages of gurus, built-in theories of self-delusion and methods of correlating its transcendent faith to wider human experience.

A second approach to the new religious movements can be found in Richard Bergeron's contribution to this issue, 'Towards a Theological Interpretation of the New Religions'. Bergeron summarily discounts neo-Orientalism and every species of occidental esotericism as gnostic monisms which involve the rejection of the sacramental, historical and dogmatic principles of Christianity. For Bergeron, the new religions embody the mystical not the ethical, knowledge not faith, protology not eschatology, experience not decision, illumination not engagement, ignorance not evil. Bergeron sees new religious movements as *simply incompatible* with Christianity.

I have several difficulties with this approach of Bergeron. My first objection involves his use of a 'typological' method which leads to over-generalisations which do not seem to fit all the facts. How he would respond to the evidence of a strongly *ethical* (not just *mystical*) component in those American Zen movements studied by Steven Tipton in his recent brilliant book on new religious movements in America is, of course, unknown. But sociological and historical studies such as Tipton's do not bear out Bergeron's essentialist reduction of these movements to 'gnostic monism'.[16]

Moreover, Bergeron's interest focuses on the ontology or soteriology of the new religious movements, not on their practice. He rightly rejects gnosticism without entertaining the question I am trying to pose in this article about the need for a Christian esoteric tradition and meditative practice which would not entail gnosticism. Such a tradition and practice could meet widespread desires—even if restricted to a definite minority of the population—for an intimate knowledge (a kind of *gnosis*) of self and self-in-transformation under the action of God.

As an alternative approach to a religious assessment of the new religious movements to those posited by 'The Spiritual Counterfeits Project' and Bergeron, I would suggest the following possible stances, on the part of the Church, to the new religious movements:

(a) Although the question of 'spiritual counterfeits' is real and pressing, we can not assume that the mere fact that a group is not Christian makes it 'a counterfeit'. We will want to find ways to distinguish between *spiritual ventures* (such as those described in the articles by Dan O'Hanlon and Robert Ellwood in this issue) and *spiritual counterfeits*.

(b) I would suggest that the most productive method to study and dialogue with new religious movements is to move from an apologetic or essentialist typological method to the comparative historical and sociological method employed so fruitfully in the History of Religions' School of comparative religious studies. This method has been helpful in suggesting both comparisons and contrasts between Christianity and other world religions. It avoids syncretism and encourages Christians in dialogue with adherents of other world religions to discover 'analogues' in their own Christian tradition (importantly *similar* and importantly *different*) to elements discovered in other world religions. Thus, I have been suggesting in this article that Christianity might find an appropriately Christian version of an esoteric tradition and practices which would avoid the dangers of the rejection of the sacramental, historical and dogmatic traditions of

Christianity. Instead of becoming crypto-Buddhist, Hindu, gnostic, etc., Christians must recover lost elements of their own experiential tradition of an 'intimate' and progressive knowledge of God. In this view, the emphasis is less on analogies to non-Christian ontologies or doctrines—as in Bergeron—and more on analogy to a practice that 'works' as a transformative inner path.

(c) As in so many other areas of change in the post-Vatican II world, the Church's attitude towards the new religious movements should shift *from anathema to dialogue*. If at some point elements in neo-Orientalism call for rejection, this should emerge not from essentialist typologies but out of dialogue with living members of neo-Orientalist groups, most of whom—as most Christians—diverge in their lived practice from any ideal-type of their religion.

(d) A Protestant theologian, Harold Wilson, has suggested the possibility of seeing the neo-Oriental cults as a 'possible preparation' for Christianity.[17] Wilson argues that there are three stages to mysticism. In the first stage, nature mysticism, individuals become aware of the affinity which unites them to the natural world around them. In this stage, they feel a sense of oneness with the created world. While this experience, at this point, might be thematised in pantheistic or monistic terms, *it is not necessary to deny the experience* in rejecting this particular thematisation of it. In a second stage, the mystic, freed from disturbing compulsions and dissipations,˙ concentrates on overcoming alienation from the self by becoming a 'centred' unity. The third stage is a distinctively Christian mysticism which leads the individual to a personal relationship with God in Christ and through that relationship to charity and service to the neighbour. In this stage the mystic becomes fully receptive to God's grace.

The three stages can be seen as progressive steps leading up to a climactic experience of the personal, loving God, the Father of Jesus. Wilson contends that it is not necessary to adopt a condemnatory attitude which would see any experience of oneness with nature as pantheistic. This first stage may be a suitable—if imperfect—way for a person with little religious training to begin his or her ascent to God. Importantly, the final stage does not eliminate the first two but rather purifies them and incorporates them into a fuller experience.

Wilson's position reminds us, again, of Needleman's basic critique of Christianity as a way of inner spiritual journey: it frequently jumps to the third stage without providing initiates with appropriate means and ideas to go through the intermediary stages. It speaks the highest language of union with God without paying attention to the preliminary steps of: (i) providing appropriate practices to tame the self-delusions and compulsions of ego; and (ii) becoming a unified self or 'soul' capable of sustained attentiveness and mindful contemplation.

(e) A fifth attitude towards the new religious movements would look upon their beliefs and practices as opportunities for growth in the knowledge and experience of analogous depths in one's own faith. Neo-Orientalist mystic-monastic movements point to the serious neglect of meditation, self-examination and discipline among Christians today.

(f) A final, related, attitude would look to the flourishing of neo-Orientalist groups as a challenge to revive a sense of 'intimate' knowledge and a flexible esoteric tradition within Christianity itself. For ultimately, Christianity proclaims that it 'works'. It promises a 'new creation', a new knowledge and a new way of being in this world. The religious challenge to Christianity by neo-Oriental religions with transformative methods of meditative practice is to become, once again, 'a way' of experience.[18]

Notes

1. For an argument that sees the new religious movements as phenomena of major religious cultural change, see Robert Wuthnow *The Consciousness Reformation* (Berkeley 1976); *New Religious Consciousness* eds. Charles Glock and Robert Bellah (Berkeley 1976); and Steven Tipton *Getting Saved From the Sixties* (Berkeley 1982).

2. For these statistics, see *Time* magazine, 3 May 1982 p. 66.

3. See Wuthnow, the work cited in note 1, p. 39, and Frederick Bird and Bill Reimer 'Participation Rates in New Religious and Para-Religious Movements' *Journal for the Scientific Study of Religion* 21, no. 1 (March 1982) 1-13.

4. Wilfred C. Smith *Toward a World Theology* (Philadelphia 1981).

5. See John A. Saliba 'A Christian Response to the New Religions' *Journal of Ecumenical Studies* 18, no. 3 (Summer 1981) 451-473.

6. Jacob Needleman *Lost Christianity* (New York 1980).

7. *Lost Christianity* p. 4.

8. *Ibid.* p. 35, italics mine.

9. *Ibid.* p. 101.

10. *Ibid.* p. 125.

11. *Ibid.* p. 87.

12. *Ibid.* p. 155, italics mine.

13. For the western antipathy to notions of hierarchy, see Louis Dumont *Homo Hierarchicus* (Chicago 1970). For a sympathetic sociological look at esoteric traditions, see *On the Margins of the Visible* ed. Edward Tiryakian (New York 1974).

14. Thomas Kasulis 'Intimacy as Heuristic Theme in Understanding Japanese Religion' unpublished paper in my possession, p. 18, italics mine.

15. Kasulis, *ibid.* p. 40, italics mine.

16. Tipton, the work cited in note 1, pp. 95-176.

17. Harold Wilson *Invasion from the East* (Minneapolis 1978) pp. 112 ff.

18. I am indebted for several of these points of an alternative response to John Saliba, in the work cited in note 5.

Robert Ellwood

Asian Religions in
North America

SPIRITUAL ASIA has long held a special fascination for English-speaking North America. While Canada and the United States have, of course, been mighty bastions of their traditional Judaeo-Christian faiths since virtually the inception of European immigration, the charm of the Other, represented by religious Asia, has also long exerted its appeal. In certain periods the Ganges has flowed into the Mississippi in torrents, dotting the floodplains with ashrams and temples.

Asian religion in North America falls into two categories: that imported by the large number of Chinese, Korean, Japanese, South East Asian, and Indian immigrants who have come to American shores; and that oriented primarily to spiritual seekers of occidental background. The temper of the two versions of Hinduism, Buddhism, Islam, and other Asiatic faiths is quite different. For the immigrants and their descendants, the religion is a quiet, familiar facet of one's identity, deeply rooted in family and ethnic community life, likely to become most prominent in such personal and family occasions as weddings and funerals. North Americans of Asian descent are, by and large, hard-working unostentatious people who, when they have not become Christian as have perhaps half, find in whatever degree of traditional religious practice they choose a faith linked to one's roots and community.

For occidentals, on the other hand, the 'journey to the East' represents a spiritual adventure with all any adventure implies: cutting familiar ties, having new experiences, finding a new community. When a religion does not have such 'given' sociological supports as family, community, and ethnic identity, then its subjective power has to be all the stronger in compensation; for this reason Asian religions catering to occidental North Americans inevitably emphasise such practices as chanting and meditation believed to induce felt spiritual experience, and tend to create intentional communities or more informal associations which offer strong subjective support through charismatic leadership and close interaction among adherents. Stress will be on the authority and power of the guru-type leader, on teaching, and on such praxis as meditation, rather than on weddings and funerals; in other words, it is on that which legitimates for one a break with one's conventional religion, and compensates for it with fresh, presumably more potent subjective experience. Our concern in this article will be with this second category of Asian religion in America.

The North American religious affair with the East has gone through several stages.

17

First, the interest was almost entirely intellectual; like some of their romanticist colleagues in Europe, the New England transcendentalists, especially Emerson and Thoreau, found in the newly-translated spiritual classics of India powerful support for their own penchant for mystical monism, and moreover found that the exotic source of that wisdom assorted well with their love of mind-expanding, far-reaching thoughts. The upshot was the 'Yankee Hindoo' mood, well expressed in the famous passage from Thoreau's *Walden* which begins:

> In the morning I bathe my intellect in the stupendous and cosmogonal philosophy of the Bhagvat-Geeta, since whose composition years of the gods have elapsed, and in comparison with which our modern world and its literature seem puny and trivial; and I doubt if that philosophy is not to be referred to a previous state of existence, so remote is its sublimity from our conceptions.[1]

The theme was taken up by the poet Walt Whitman, who sang in his 1871 poem 'Passage to India' of

> Passage O soul to India!

and then

> Passage to more than India!
> O secret of the earth and sky!

suggesting that for such souls India was really what it has always been for many seekers, not so much a geographical place as a state of mind and a sublime mystical high ground of which the hot, teeming country was only symbol and starting-point.

The quest went beyond such musings to take concrete sociological expression with the formation of the Theosophical Society in New York in 1875, by the Russian-born Helena P. Blavatsky and the American Henry Steel Olcott, to explore the ancient wisdom underlying all religion and philosophy, both eastern and western. It early developed a special interest in India as a reservoir of such lore, however, and by 1879 the two founders had arrived there. Despite many vicissitudes, Theosophy has played a significant role in introducing eastern ideas into western popular culture and in holding up spiritual Asia as a positive magnet of the soul.

The World Parliament of Religions held in Chicago in 1893 gave a new impetus to Asiatic religions. The dramatic Swami Vivekananda made an impression out of which came the Ramakrishna Mission's American centres, commonly known as Vedanta Societies, which have particularly attracted intellectuals to Indic thought, and spiritual guidance by its swamis. The Japanese Zen monk Soyen Shaku was also present and later (in 1905) began formal Zen work in America with several students. The well-known lay writer on Zen, D. T. Suzuki, also a student of Soyen Shaku, first lived near Chicago, 1897-1909, as a translator and writer.

Zen did not 'catch on' as readily as Theosophy and Vedanta, however, for which soil had been well prepared by the Transcendentalists and their kin. The pre-First World War era of occidental orientalism can be characterised as putting greatest emphasis on verbal communication. Groups from that generation still appear laden with books and lectures, and their meetings or services still evidence continuity with the liberal Protestantism of their Transcendentalist fathers in faith. The Theosophical or Vedanta Society meeting is likely to be a Sunday lecture in a plain hall with few symbolic ornaments but plenty of books on display.

In the period between the wars, a new set of groups appeared which shared the basic premises of the older, but showed a freer, more expansive and more praxis-oriented style, usually centred on a flamboyant, charismatic personality. The Self-Realisation Fellowship of Swami Yogananda, the Krishnamurti enthusiasm in Theosophy, the 'I Am' offshot of Theosophy, the Meher Baba movement, and the First Zen Institute in New York all typify this era. With them there is less reading and more doing, fewer didactic lectures and more warm relationship with a remarkable personality.

Finally, after the Second World War, and especially in the Sixties, another style appeared taking the tendency of the Twenties and Thirties much further. North America was now ready, indeed eager, to accept eastern imports unadulterated. Many gladly adopted the dress, diet, and worship of new faiths' alien homelands, frequently eager to express alienation from the whole of western culture. It was a period which saw the exfoliation of Krishna Consciousness, Zen centres, Subud, and many yoga and esoteric Buddhist groups bringing a new and colourful diversity to American streets.

We shall now survey the major Asian religions in North America in terms of place of origin, starting with India and moving eastwards. As we have seen, movements of Hindu background have been the oldest and have had a general influence shared only by that of Zen. The first were the Vedanta Societies of the Ramakrishna Mission, followed in 1920 by the Self-Realisation Fellowship. In the post-war era several more yoga-teaching groups, most in the tradition of the great Swami Sivananda, appeared: the Integral Yoga Institute, the Sivananda Yoga Society, the Yasodhara Ashram Society in British Columbia. These typically have a small, often monastic core of highly committed disciples, and offer yoga classes and instruction to a much larger public.

By far the most successful numerically of Hindu-based groups has been the Transcendental Meditation movement of Maharishi Mahesh Yogi, which teaches a simple method of meditation, said not to be explicitly religious though based on Advaita Vedanta philosphical premises and involving a certain rite of initiation. It claims to have initiated over a million Americans into its practice; many of course were also members of other religious bodies, and not all persisted in the use, but the career of 'TM' in North America has been remarkable, clearly indicating some spiritual need unmet by the traditional religions.

The 1960s and 1970s saw the rise, and sometimes fall, of a number of movements centred on particular Hindu gurus who ventured West. One of the most celebrated was the Divine Light Mission of the teenage Guru Maharaj Ji, which reported some 50,000 followers in its heyday but declined after internal dissent. At the time of writing, the Siddha Yoga of Swami Muktananda is acquiring a large following. Guru movements like these are characteristically heralded by reports of remarkable initiatory experiences imparted by the guru himself, worship with him or under his power which engenders strong, electrifying feeling, and a mobile group of western disciples who spend time at the guru's headquarters in India as well as with him in the West. The recent trend seems to be towards popular gurus in the Tantric tradition, as indicated by Muktananda and the growing vogue for Shree Rajneesh.

Most Hindu movements in North America have, broadly speaking, come out of the Vedanta tradition which emphasises realising the divine within through yoga and meditation techniques. The devotional exception to this is the highly visible International Society for Krishna Consciousness. Communalistic and a total way of life for core devotees, it inculcates bhaktic worship of Krishna as a personal deity, the 'supreme personality of Godhead'.

Several movements of Sikh background have had some success among occidental North Americans. The Sikh Dharma, established in America by Yogi Bhajan, who also teaches 'kundalini yoga' through the related 3HO ('Healthy, Happy, Holy Organisation'), has some 5,000 adherents who live in ashrams and dress in a conspicuous Sikh manner. Radhasoami Satsang and Ruhani Satsang, related Sikh sectarian movements, have also been brought to America.

Moving to South East Asia, we find that relatively few occidentals have established groups and movements around Theravada Buddhism, although interest seems to be growing, especially in vipassana meditation. A number of people have gone to Sri Lanka, Burma, or Thailand to study it and returned to write and lecture. An interesting movement is Subud, founded by an Indonesian called Bapak and undoubtedly inspired by Sufi practices. Its major practice, the Latihan, gives the total release of entering a room with other members of the same sex and doing whatever one is moved to do—shouting, jumping, singing.

Similarly, we find very few religious movements of Chinese origin in North America. There is a great deal of interest in philosophical Taoism and Ch'an Buddhism among spiritual seekers, but usually it is precisely the allegedly unstructured spirituality of those traditions that draws them, and those souls do not find it necessary to form a group to walk in the woods meditating on the *Tao Te Ching* or the *Platform Sutra*. If a formal community and a teaching lineage is desired, its expression in Japanese Zen seems more accessible, even though Zen was itself transmitted from China to medieval Japan. However, the Sino-American Buddhist Association of San Francisco, with its Gold Mountain Monastery and its rural City of Ten Thousand Buddhas, has drawn some occidental followers, including some who have become monks and nuns, despite a highly conservative and rigorous approach.

Tibet and its Vajrayana Buddhism, on the other hand, are coming more and more into view. While actual numbers of serious occidental Vajrayanists may be small, the colour, strangeness, difficulty, and alleged power and profundity of this tradition are a challenge some seekers cannot resist. The Nyingmapa Center in Berkeley (California) teaches a traditional regimen of Tibetan practice. Conversely, the growing Vajradhatu movement, headquartered in Boulder (Colorado), is quite eclectic, promoting experimentation with spiritual paths. Programmes at its Nalanda University have been widely influential in the American eastern religious world.

We come now to Japan. Three of the Japanese 'New Religions', doctrinally monotheist and oriented towards healing and an optimistic eschatology, but more Shinto than Buddhist in style of worship, have attracted a small but perhaps significant occidental following: Tenrikyo, Perfect Liberty, and World Messianity. Larger numbers, however, have been attracted to two modern movements based in Nichiren Buddhism, Rissho Kosei Kai and, above all, Soka Gakkai, the dynamic and controversial lay organisation affiliated with Nichiren Shoshu. Established in North America as the Nichiren Shoshu Academy, the latter grew dramatically in the late 1960s and early 1970s, claiming as many as 200,000 adherents who had installed its household altar, the Gohonzon, and presumably recited the chant, *Nam myoho renge kyo*, which for Nichiren Buddhism is the key to power. As in Japan, North American Nichiren Shoshu is a modernised, youth-oriented movement noted for busy promotional activity, popular music concerts, and effervescent conventions. However, as in Japan it seems to have declined since a high point in the early 1970s.

Zen has unquestionably had the greatest cultural influence in North America of any form of Buddhism. From the poetry and prose of the 1950s 'Beat Generation' to the music of John Cage, not to mention Zen's inevitable connection with any love of traditional Japanese painting, gardens, or architecture, Zen has left its stamp on American life and letters. We shall examine the career of Zen in America in some detail as an example of how the spiritual Orient has found its place on western shores.

American Zen has two interlocking wings: the formal Zen of Zen centres under the guidance of a Japanese-trained *roshi* or master, where regular zazen or seated Zen meditation is taught and practised; and what might be called informal (or, in the Fifties' term, Beat), Zen, the Zen of assorted poets, artists, and wanderers for whom it has represented freedom and spontaneity. (In China and Japan, too, both wings have long been known.) The first wing, as we have seen, goes back to early in the century, but was firmly established only in 1930 when the First Zen Institute of America was founded in New York, with Shigemitsu Sasaki, a student of a student of Soyen Shaku, as *roshi*. Other formal Zen centres, some from out of different lineages of Japanese masters, were established, mostly during the 1960s.

The ground for the level of zeal for Zen which led to the presence of some two dozen Zen centres in the United States and Canada by the end of that decade was prepared in the late Forties and the Fifties. One factor was the American occupation of Japan after the war; not a few of those who were to plant Zen in America first encountered it as GIs in the defeated nation. Another was the writing, and the lecturing in America in that period, of the tireless D. T. Suzuki, and of another writer and speaker who learned most of what he knew of Zen from Suzuki, the transplanted Englishman Alan Watts. Both favoured the romantic, spontaneous, quasi-Taoist style of Zen over the monastic, and both communicated it with ease and wit in book after book.

A first-fruits of their labours was the role of Zen in the Beat culture, especially around San Francisco, of the 1950s. It was chronicled by the novelist Jack Kerouac in *The Dharma Bums*, and deeply influences the poetry of Gary Snyder, who appears in the novel thinly disguised as Japhy Ryder, the ideal young American poet, outdoorsman, and Zennist. His coterie explicitly sought to emulate the 'Zen Lunatics' of old China and Japan by living lives dedicated to freedom, unconventionality, experience, and closeness to nature.

The two wings connect, however. Alan Watts's first mother-in-law was Ruth Fuller Everett, patron of the First Zen Institute who, widowed, married Sasaki Roshi in 1944. After his death only a year later, she settled in Japan, where she became a notable Zen scholar and priest of a small temple in the great Daitokuji complex in Kyoto; there she befriended many young Americans, including Gary Snyder, who came to Japan to study Zen.

Finally, we must note that Zen takes its place as but one manifestation of the longstanding American tradition of a way of life which loves nature, lives unconventionally, and feels an affinity for the Orient. This tradition goes back to the Transcendentalists and was earlier expressed in Theosophy; the American Zennists, often quite self-consciously, saw themselves as part of that heritage. Alan Watts first learned of Zen and met Suzuki through the British Buddhist and Theosophist Christmas Humphreys; Suzuki's American wife, Beatrice Lane Suzuki, was an active Theosophist herself. Kerouac was an avid reader of Thoreau who dreamed of going somewhere to live the Walden life; instead he discovered Zen.

The spiritual East in North America, then, while more visible in some times and places than others, is a deeply-rooted and inseparable part of American culture.

Note

1. Henry David Thoreau *Walden* (New York 1942) p. 198. Originally published in 1854.

Bibliography

Bellah, Robert N., and Glock, Charles Y., eds. *The New Religious Consciousness* (Berkeley, University of California Press, 1976).

Bridges, Hal *American Mysticism: From William James to Zen* (New York, Harper & Row, 1970).

Ellwood, Robert S. *Alternative Altars: Unconventional and Eastern Spirituality in America* (Chicago, University of Chicago Press, 1979).

Ellwood, Robert S. *The Eagle and the Rising Sun: Americans and the New Religions of Japan* (Philadelphia, Westminster Press, 1974).

Ellwood, Robert S. *Religious and Spiritual Groups in Modern America* (Englewood Cliffs, NJ, Prentice-Hall, 1973).

Judah, J. Stillson *Hare Krishna and the Counter Culture* (New York, John Wiley & Sons, 1974).

Needleman, Jacob *The New Religions* (Garden City, NY, Doubleday, 1970).

Prebish, Charles S. *American Buddhism* (North Scituate, MA, Duxberry Press, 1979).

Reinhart Hummel and Bert Hardin

Asiatic Religions in Europe

THE RELIGIOUS groups with a Hindu or Buddhist background that reached Europe in the 1960s and 1970s[1] came without exception by way of the United States and thus penetrated the Old World in an 'Americanised' form. The aspects that struck people as objectionable—the commercialisation, the PR methods, etc.—were North American rather than Asian characteristics. Several features, such as the attempt of Transcendental Meditation to present itself as a purely secular technique of relaxation, were connected with the strict separation of Church and State in the USA and would probably not have come into being at all in Europe. To this extent the fact that these cults reached Europe via the USA worked against their chances of success. This makes it all the more interesting to study a movement which may have been strongly influenced by the psychological climate in North America but which nevertheless reached Europe directly from India. This is the movement led by Bhagwan Shree Rajneesh. This study will therefore focus on this movement as it is representative of more recent trends in the religious scene.

Typical meditation movements like TM and the Divine Light Mission had by the middle of the 1970s passed their peak and have since entered on a phase of consolidation. One reason for this has been the campaign against youth cults and sects which was able to uncover a whole series of internal contradictions. What was involved above all was the gulf between claim and reality. These groups not only showed themselves incapable of fulfilling the almost paradisiacal promises they made: the techniques of meditation themselves that they used were often shown to be dangerous and sometimes lacking in intellectual and spiritual content. Many leading members remained discontented and found fulfilment in movements of a more strongly Hindu character such as that led by Sathya Sai Baba.

The diffuse influence of non-organised forms of Asiatic spirituality such as yoga and Zen is, moreover, a characteristic of the intellectual and spiritual climate. Perhaps the dying out of humanist education is a reason for a monist attitude to life no longer relying on quotations from Goethe today but on passages from the Upanishads or from Buddhist writings.

Of recent years the focus has shifted from the soul to the body and geographically from India to China and Japan. What are sought today are techniques that serve the body's physical self-awareness and development such as T'ai Chi Ch'uan and Aikido. Bringing body and soul into harmony is meant to mobilise the primeval energy of the cosmos and enable one to experience it. This means that the time is also ripe for the dervish dances from the Islamic Sufi movement and Tantra yoga with its Hindu and Buddhist origins. Tantra yoga includes the body and sexuality in the process of salvation. There is also an increase in interest in Tibetan Buddhism with its Tantric influences.

1. THE BHAGWAN MOVEMENT[2]

It is above all the Neo-Sanya movement led by Bhagwan Shree Rajneesh, at first in Poona but since 1981 in Antelope, Oregon, that bids fair to rival the Volkswagen Beetle: it runs and runs. Far from indicating the end and dissolution of the movement, the breaking up of the ashram in Poona introduced a new phase in its spread by bringing about the return to Europe and the United States of the élite of therapists and committed staff members. By 1981 the number of Rajneesh centres in Belgium had risen to seven, in France to eleven, in Great Britain to twenty-six, in Italy to eighteen, in the Netherlands to twenty-five, and in West Germany to fifty-seven. In Germany, on which our investigation will now focus, the movement's centre of gravity will in the future be the newly acquired Wolfsbrunnen castle in Meinhard-Schwebda. Here a city of Rajneesh is planned, an enormous centre for therapy and growth with an abundance of handicrafts and similar opportunities for the sannyasis to translate their devotion to their master into actual work.

Previously the largest German Rajneesh Meditation Centre was Purvodaya in Margarethenried north-east of Munich. According to its own figures this 'centre for self-awareness and meditation' has shown the following increase in turnover: 1978, DM 205,000 (nearly £48,000); 1979, DM 725,000 (nearly £170,000); 1980, DM 2,632,000 (over £600,000); while that budgeted for 1981 was nearly five million deutschmarks (over £1,150,000). Sixty-seven per cent of the visitors were between 20 and 29 years old and 14 per cent between 30 and 39, with the rest being older or younger. Eighty per cent were classified as middle class (the majority teachers and students, very many from the field of social work, with the rest being officials and white-collar and manual workers). There is a certain noticeable tendency for leading members to be drawn from the aristocracy. Many of the newly opened centres operate under names drawn from the field of humanist psychology. They cannot be immediately recognised as Rajneesh centres. While the castle and its grounds have apparently been acquired for the new city of Rajneesh by the Rajneesh Foundation, most of the centres are independent. Their cohesion is guaranteed by the attitude of discipleship towards the master Bhagwan Shree Rajneesh on the part of those running them. Looked at from the point of view of organisation, the Neo-Sanya movement does not fit into the pattern of youth cults and sects among which it is often counted. Its organisational structure is heirarchical but not totalitarian. Many visitors to the Rajneesh centres come because of the therapeutic groups and leave when and how they want. Alongside these Bhagwan clients there are also Bhagwan believers for whom Rajneesh is a second Buddha or Jesus. This fits in with the fluctuating character of this movement which is at one and the same time a psycho-religious movement, a syncretistic guru-cult and an esoteric school of the mysteries.

2. RAJNEESH: FROM REBEL TO GURU

Born in 1931, Rajneesh began his career not as the guru of a predominantly western flock of disciples but as a radical critic of his own culture, as a 'lonely enlightened rebel' (R. C. Prasad) against the taboos of Indian politics and religion. His official biography, however, mentions religious experiences during childhood and an experience of enlightenment when he was a student at the age of twenty-one. Obviously he went on to experiment with techniques of meditation and similar techniques of altering one's awareness and from 1964 onwards introduced his followers to these in meditation camps in Rajasthan. Here, too, he did not follow the usual pattern. He did not teach the usual forms of yoga but predominantly group meditation and dances that had been developed by Gurdjieff, probably relying on Sufi traditions. Parallel to his appropriation of new concepts and practices, a change came about in his own appraisal of himself. Up till the 1960s he was known to the Indian public as Acharya (teacher) Rajneesh: he finally became Bhagwan (God) and thus one of mankind's great enlightened ones. With this should be connected the withdrawal from public life that led to the foundation of an ashram first in Bombay (1969) and later in Poona (1974 to 1981).

While Rajneesh was still teaching philosophy, Michael Murphy and Richard Price founded the Esalen Centre in California in 1962. With its remarkable blend of western psychology and eastern wisdom it was the model of other 'human growth centres'. It was at Esalen that Fritz Perls, the founder of Gestalt psychology, came to rest in his old age; the pupil of Wilhelm Reich and the founder of bio-energetics, Alexander Lowen, and his pupil Stanley Keleman worked there; there too Alan Watts, the champion of Beat Zen, and Baba Ram Dass, alias Dr Richard Alpert, the former colleague of the apostle of LSD Timothy Leary, were able to teach their philosophies and practices inspired by the East. Towards the end of the 1960s the first European 'growth centres' appeared in London and Amsterdam, and in them the name of Rajneesh first began to be secretly whispered. It was from these places and from German psychological centres such as ZIST and AAO that an increasing number of professional and lay therapists as well as adherents of this kind of psychological culture found their way first to Bombay and later to Poona. The first generation of people who today are aged around thirty-five[3] had for the most part experimented with LSD and similar drugs as well as with techniques of altering consciousness, and were acquainted with the ideas of Gurdjieff, Reich and others. For them what they were able to experience at the feet of Rajneesh was the crowning fulfilment of all their previous searching. Rajneesh, who from his reading was already familiar with the concepts of humanist psychology, had for his part no hesitation over enlisting in his service western therapists and even artists like Georg Deuter and thus turning his ashram in Poona into 'the greatest human growth centre of the world', as it liked to describe itself. To the extent that techniques of humanist psychology found acceptance, the Rajneesh ashram became more attractive for Europeans and North Americans. In the second half of the 1970s this development led to the ashram becoming westernised. There was an appreciable diminution in the part played by Indians, and perhaps it was ultimately only consistent for Rajneesh to move to the USA in 1981.

3. THE BHAGWAN MOVEMENT AS A PSYCHO-RELIGIOUS MOVEMENT

Most seekers arrive at the Bhagwan centres because they 'have problems' or want to 'change' themselves; after taking part for a shorter or longer period of time in the work of the groups and the meditation exercises they return to their normal occupations. In the introductory phase the function of the groups and the meditation exercises is above all to clear up unresolved conflicts and 'unfinished business', to liberate blocked energies and let them flow once more. In Rajneesh's monistic interpretation of the world there is fundamentally only one energy which in the sense of humanist psychology he is able to call 'bio-energy'. It is 'life' itself or 'love' or even the 'light'. Most practices and rituals of meditation are aimed at making it possible to experience this energy and become aware of it. The dance meditations, known as 'stop techniques', that Rajneesh had taken over from Gurdjieff, do this by following phases of extreme physical exertion and hectic ecstasy by complete rest. An important ritual is the energy *darshan* that in traditional Indian terminology is called *shaktipat*, that is the transmission of power by touch or glance. The ceremony of initiation or dedication includes, besides handing over the *mala*, the wooden chain with Rajneesh's portrait, a transmission of energy of this kind by pressing the thumb on the so-called third eye. The mobilisation and experience of energy is also the aim of Buddhist exercises intended to increase one's attention and of Chinese physical techniques like T'ai Chi.

This conscious awareness of one's inner life ('Let it happen . . .') is meant to help people to distance themselves from it. Eventually they become neutral, uninvolved, impartially observing 'witnesses'—the *sahshi* of classical Indian yoga. Awareness understood in this sense is a key to understanding Rajneesh's thought: it does not matter whether someone renounces sexuality[4] or 'accepts' it. Both lead to the goal, as long as it happens with awareness. A concept taken from the vocabulary of western psychology is thus interpreted by Rajneesh against the background of Hindu and Buddhist ideas and elevated to become the supreme value.

The stream of energy that has been liberated by group work and meditation and is now consciously perceived has its origin, according to Rajneesh, in the sexual centre, the *muladhara chakra* of the physiology of Tantra yoga. Most people are so 'deformed' by religious prejudices and social pressures that their energy is 'perverted'. But 'perverted energy cannot be transformed'. Hence the importance of the introductory phase in which the individual should learn to overcome his or her inhibitions and to let the stream of energy flow. Rajneesh recommends the Tantric way: acceptance and surrender. Because 'spirituality and sexuality are two ends of one and the same energy', one and the same business is involved in the mutual surrender of man and woman as in the relation of master and disciple. The relationship of the disciple to the master is a 'relationship of love'. Like Tantrism as a whole, Rajneesh has a divided attitude towards sexuality. On the one hand he stresses with tremendous anti-puritan emphasis, the divinity of the unique power of life; on the other he stresses the necessity for it to be transformed and transcended. What happens in practice is an increasing depersonalisation of sexual relations, which is clearly experienced by many people who are plagued by problems of personal relationships as a liberating break-through to the knowledge that everyone is irrevocably alone and must learn not to need anyone else. Corresponding to this is the repeated emphasis on everyone being exclusively responsible for himself or herself and for his or her inner development.

What stops people surrendering themselves in trust to the master and to the stream of life he personifies is the 'mind'. The 'mind' enables us to plan for the future or to play the 'games' of the past and keeps us from living with full awareness in the here and now. Following Gurdjieff, Rajneesh emphasises that the unawakened man or woman is only reacting like an automaton instead of living authentically on the basis of his or her own spontaneity.

4. THE BHAGWAN MOVEMENT AS A SYNCRETISTIC GURU-CULT

Rajneesh does not see himself as a guru in the traditional sense of the word, and in fact he is not one. Nevertheless certain ritual elements of honouring the guru are maintained in the Rajneesh centres: the main feasts are Rajneesh's birthday and the day of his enlightenment as well as Guru-purnima, the feast of the full moon. But Rajneesh is not to be equated with the guarantor of a particular doctrinal tradition since doctrinal traditions are something he fundamentally rejects. Even in Poona personal contact with his followers was reduced to a very low level and has ceased almost entirely with his move to the United States. In this way he pays no attention to many functions ascribed to the guru by the classical tradition. Nevertheless his person assumes an extraordinarily important role in the life of his followers. To begin with, the master is for Rajneesh the object of that surrender without which it is impossible to overcome the ego and 'mind'. The erotic and sexual character of this surrender is clear to those affected: it is not by accident that Satyananda uses the metaphor 'becoming intimate with the master'.

A consistent trait in Rajneesh's understanding of the master's function is his stress on absolute passivity: 'No relationship exists on the part of the master because the master does not exist. . . . If your ego is there, project it too on to the master. It is your projection.[5] What Rajneesh is describing is the condition of the person who is fully enlightened. The connection between his reinterpretation of the Buddhist ideal and his presentation of himself as a screen for people to project their ideas on to is unambiguous. Hence there is no lack of statements to the effect that the master's voice is fundamentally 'my own inner voice'. Even Rajneesh's physical absence does not make any essential difference to this kind of relationship between master and disciple.

The trust that is continually demanded in the master characterises the atmosphere in the Bhagwan centres and above all the work in the therapeutic groups. Readiness to abandon oneself to what happens in the group and to give up every kind of usual safeguard is demanded and guaranteed on the basis of trust in Bhagwan's omnipresence. This means, too, a substantial reduction in the burden of responsibility borne by the therapist: he or she can stop worrying about professional prudence because Bhagwan is responsible for everything.

Seeing himself as an 'enlightened master' also characterises Rajneesh's dealings with the religious traditions of mankind. He has indeed used the sacred writings of the most diverse religions as the basis for his lectures: from the Buddhist world a handful of *mahayana sutras* and above all the literature of Zen, from the Chinese world a series of Taoist writings, from the Indian tradition some of the later Upanishads, Patanjali's yoga sutras, Tantric writings, the songs of the Bengali Baul, and especially the writings of Kabir, and in addition he draws on Sufic and Hasidic writings. It is thus above all the mystics of the different religious traditions that are expounded for his hearers and readers, admittedly in Rajneesh's uniform interpretation; and this in itself is an astonishing expansion of the usual western intellectual horizon that certainly accounts for part of Rajneesh's attraction. Of course, in Rajneesh's interpretation they are all saying the same thing, with certain nuances. Similarly, this brilliant assimilator, as R. C. Prasad calls him, slips easily into the role of the Zen master, of the Sufi sheikh, of the Hasidic rabbi, and above all into that of the great founders of religion like Buddha and Jesus. What they said of themselves ('I am the way', etc.) are transformed almost without being noticed into statements by Rajneesh about himself, and his relationship to his followers covertly becomes the main theme of the history of religion. Fundamentally he is not the source of any new religious ideas. It is not a new idea but Rajneesh himself as the enlightened one and as master around whom the fullness of the various religious traditions syncretistically form themselves. To this extent one is justified in describing the Bhagwan movement as a syncretistic guru-cult. The idea that as an enlightened one Rajneesh is talking 'on the same level' as Buddha and Jesus serves as a legitimation for interpretations that depart from traditional ones. This is of course particulary the case with regard to the Semitic traditions.

5. THE BHAGWAN MOVEMENT AS AN ESOTERIC SCHOOL OF THE MYSTERIES

A fundamental principle with Rajneesh is that demands for faith are to be rejected and that all statements must be based on experience alone. Hence in his circle it is only with a certain uneasiness and an embarrassed smile that people admit to believing in karma and reincarnation and other esoteric doctrines. Clearly there are hopes of oneself reaching, under Rajneesh's guidance, the status of an enlightened one.[6] 'The ashram is a nursery in which enlightened ones are produced, and Bhagwan is the chief incubator.' Connected with this are hopes of cosmic proportions, because with an increasing number of enlightened ones the 'entire state of vibration of the planet' is altered. In connection with certain astrological constellations of the 1980s and the hope that the 'age of Aquarius' is about to dawn, there arise expectations of a 'quantum leap' on the part of mankind and its being saved from a catastrophe of apocalyptic proportions. Against the background of the belief that Rajneesh was a great Tibetan master who lived seven centuries ago and has now returned in order to gather his former pupils around him once again, the traditional greetings used by Rajneesh, such as: 'Here you are at last' or: 'I've been waiting for you for a long time', take on a deeper meaning. Also to be included among these esoteric speculations are Rajneesh's statements about Hitler as a tool of the Great White Brotherhood who unfortunately ended by making himself independent and was thus the cause of the ruin of the Second World War. Clearly there are more speculations of this kind circulating around Rajneesh than have hitherto been made public.

In order to understand this fluctuating phenomenon as a whole it is important to bear in mind the wealth of different aspects under which Rajneesh presents himself. The traditions of West and East combine to provide a stream of water to drive his greedy mills. He has succeeded in satisfying equally such disparate needs as that for psychological relief and enrichment, that for the religious experience of being dissolved into oneness with the ground of all being, and that for the attainment of esoteric secret knowledge. He has succeeded in presenting himself in the role of the psychological healer, the religiously enlightened one, and the great initiate and adept. The boundaries between these different roles are fluid, and equally fluid are the distinctions among his followers. Alongside the great mass of Bhagwan clients is the band of Bhagwan believers for whom Rajneesh has become the symbol and embodiment of cosmic life and love, and finally there is the élite of those who have been initiated into the mysteries of the cosmos and its future. In the immense market-place of religions and pseudo-religions on offer there are at the moment no rivals who can cover so broad a spectrum of expectations and needs.

Translated by Robert Nowell

Notes

1. See Reinhart Hummel *Indische Mission und neue Frömmigkeit im Westen* (Stuttgart 1981).
2. See R. C. Prasad *Rajneesh: The Mystic of Feeling* (Delhi ²1978).
3. See the seven interviews in Swami Satyananda *Im Grunde ist alles ganz einfach* (Frankfurt 1981). (Satyananda is the monastic name of Jörg-Andrees Elten, formerly well-known as a reporter on *Stern* magazine.) This also includes references to further literature.
4. For Rajneesh's attitude to sexuality see above all Bhagwan Shree Rajneesh *Book of the Secrets, vol. 2: Discourses on Vigyana Bhairava Tantra* (Poona 1975).
5. Bhagwan Shree Rajneesh *Mein Weg. Der Weg der weissen Wolke* (Berlin, no date) p. 261.
6. For what follows, see Swami Satyananda, the work cited in note 3 pp. 128 f., 116 ff.

Daniel O'Hanlon

A View of the US Scene from Asia Through American Eyes

BACK IN 1973 and again in 1976 I travelled in India and some of the principal Buddhist countries with a view to gaining first-hand experience of Hindu and Buddhist religious life and practice. Along the way I ran into hundreds of young westerners who were on the move, in search of something, and had many conversations with them. After my return to the States, reflecting on these many conversations which had simply happened unplanned, the idea came to me of spending a couple of months systematically interviewing these westerners in Asia.

I finally narrowed down my focus to those who had grown up in the United States. Learning how, from their new perspective, they viewed the land they grew up in might, I thought, shed some light on the so-called new religious phenomenon in the United States. So in the summer of 1978, with the competent assistance of David Hackett, a young graduate student, I visited India, Nepal and Thailand and ended up with seventy taped interviews, about an hour and a half each, with Americans in Asia. This short article can deal with only a fraction of that rich material, and it has been difficult for me to find a way to do it justice in such limited space. The kind of consensus that emerges from all seventy of these Americans should not be neglected. Yet much of the value and interest of the interviews lies in their concrete personal detail. But to give detailed accounts of even a few of them here is clearly not possible. I will present only two of the interviews, then, and even those only in abbreviated form. I will next present some observations and generalisations based on these two and on the whole sample of seventy. The two I have chosen are a Buddhist nun in Thailand and a Hindu sadhu who lives in India.

Joseph was the first American we ran into in the streets of Katmandu. We interviewed him as he sat crosslegged on the floor of his small hut near Swayambu, an ancient temple on the outskirts of Katmandu. We found that he had been eleven or twelve years in Asia, with several return visits to the States along the way. His home base is in Bengal, India, where he has his own ashram and runs a clinic, quite a contrast to the life for which his family had prepared him.

'I grew up during the depression with the religion of capitalism. My family knew they had to make a buck to survive. All our table conversation as I was growing up was about money: how to make money and how to operate in the financial world. We were very Reformed Jewish. Although we had almost no religious practice we were a really close

29

family, because we grew up working together. That was our whole life and there wasn't time for anything else. And I'm deeply grateful to my father who gave me and my two brothers the capacity to move and take care of ourselves anywhere in the world.'

When he had finished his studies in law and accounting and had the law exams behind him, he did the conventional European tour. Sitting in Amsterdam at Het Dam Square with his return ticket to the United States, 'I met a scraggly-looking American with a beard, a sleeping bag and a guitar. No shoes. He showed me his passport and it read like a novel. Yet he had been at one time a vice-president of engineering for Litton Industries. Well, by the end of the conversation he had my ticket to the United States and I had his sleeping bag. After that I began to travel instead of tour. First Europe, but no longer in fancy hotels, then Malta, Africa, and overland to India via Turkey and Afghanistan. All along what attracted me most were the monasteries and mosques.

'And what intrigued me about all these religious people and groups was that it was an alternative to the economic way of life. I grew up with the religion of capitalism and here was something entirely different. Here they were, talking about loving God; there was no profit in it. And I couldn't understand. I remember an amazing non-stop two-day conversation with a sadhu in India. Finally I asked him: "Well, what do you *do*? I mean, how do you have so much time to spend just sitting around rapping and philosophising and thinking all these great thoughts? What do you *DO*?" And he said, "Well, I'm a sadhu. I'm a monk." And it was a whole new concept to me meeting people whose occupation it was to philosophise, to think, to meditate. It was so different from the concept that time is money. It made a tremendous impression on me.'

Joseph spent six months in Afghanistan, earning money by bringing tourists to a local carpet seller, and learning the practice of zikhr in a mosque. He ended his overland journey to India in Kashmir, in north-west India, found a teacher, Laxnmanjool, and stayed with him for five months. This was the beginning of his fascination with Sanskrit texts, not principally as doctrinal sources, but as vehicles for prayerful meditation and practice. He spends a lot of time with the Sanskrit scriptures. 'No translation is like the experience of going through a sutra syllable by syllable, in the original Sanskrit, and suddenly feeling the intensity of the vibration. If it isn't an intuitive experience, it doesn't take away your ordinary calculating mind. It's just a philosophical explanation.' This opening into the spiritual world of Hinduism came only gradually, however. Even after the five months with Laxmanjool, he felt he still had a 'western mind'. As he moved on, he hitched a ride on a poor man's houseboat hauling lumber from north of Srinagar. The boatman was pushing the boat, and Joseph asked him, 'Wouldn't you like a motor for your boat?' And he answered, 'What for? It makes so much noise. I push the boat—I look at the beauty of nature.' Joseph asked, 'Well, wouldn't you like a pair of shoes?' He replied 'Well, if I covered my feet with shoes, I'd separate them from the earth, and then I'd ask foolish questions like you do'.

'But the real turning point for me in my experience of Asia was moving into a village and buying a Hindi grammar. Learning Hindi opened up a whole new world of experience to me. Now I could communicate with the holy men and spiritual seekers on the road. Hindi was the key which put me in touch with all kinds of teachers: teachers of yoga, of philosophy, of asanas, of meditation. I find that yoga asanas are very necessary to put the body in condition. If the body cannot sit still then it is impossible to make the mind sit still. And learning Hindi made me disinclined to associate with western tourists. In fact, I've reached the point where Hindi and Sanskrit are more my mother tongue than English.'

'Another thing I discovered is that there's a gulf between philosophers and practitioners. You find that village people in their simplicity, in the daily devotions they take for granted, are closer to living the ideal than the university professors. Go and live with them. You'll be amazed at the generosity and openness with which interested seekers are received. I found that when I just looked at cultures a a tourist, I formed very superficial opinions. When I sat down with the people and practised what they practised, and tried to do what they do and eat and live the way they lived, every door in the village opened.'

'What about the States?' I asked, 'Have you been back for visits?' 'Yes, four times over the last twelve years. Three times I stayed ninety days each, mostly building houses to replenish my finances. The last time I stayed a full year and with that money I built my ashram in Bengal, the clinic, and a Sanskrit institute. My parents would prefer that I become a capitalist or own an empire in the West. But they've come to accept my way of life, and my father came over five years ago to see what I gave up all that stuff in the West for. We made a deal. I said I would travel half the time first class with him if he would travel half the time as a sadhu with me. And he did. Said he had only two weeks to spend and he ended up staying over a month and a half. By the letters I get from him I wouldn't be surprised if he eventually retired to the ashram with me.'

Joseph had some very positive things to say about his American upbringing: 'With that Yankee ingenuity we can come and get it together anywhere in the world because of our wide range of experience. We've *seen* things. Seen so many things that people with lesser developed communications, and less education, even the Europeans, haven't had. That's a tremendous advantage. But it's also a disadvantage, because we're not taught how to turn the machine off. And when it comes time to sit quietly, generally the only remedy in the West is television or the movies, where we can vegetate for a few hours and involve our psyche in some trite little drama that's going on before us. So we lose our ego-I that's been running all this time. But it's not really quiet. Unfortunately that same American energy is very much in demand in India today. I think a time will even come when the East will have to go to the West to find its heritage.

'Another thing about America is that religious education is very very lacking. I was barmitzvahed at thirteen but it didn't mean anything to me. My main criticism of religion in America is the emphasis on fund raising, whether it's the mainline religions or groups like TM or Hare Krishna. They're all out hawking their wares. But religion is not to be sold. It's to be given and shared in peace, and its harmony and its love and its way of life! There are tremendous structural differences. The Hindu faiths allow for religious seekers. They allow for their independence. Western religions don't allow independence. You are either one of the fold, or you're a lost sheep. But in India you can travel about as a wandering ascetic and go to any monastery, any temple, sit down, chant the worship, whatever you want to chant. Sometimes I pray in Hebrew, sometimes in Arabic. I'm allowed that scope and I'm not considered a lost sheep. People come and say. "Gee! That was beautiful! What were you chanting?" And I say, "Well, that was Talmud", and they're very curious. They want to know. But when I stayed in Greek Orthodox monasteries or in the Hebrew Yeshiva, for instance, there was regimentation. I had to be at their prayer at 5:30 a.m. and was supposed to say so many verses of set text. No freedom to work out my spiritual practice. But no one can tell you how sweet your tea should be.

'Myself, I really dig what I'm doing. Lots of ups and downs, but I take them all in my stride. I don't really consider myself religious in the classical sense of the term. The Hindi sect I've been initiated into worships life and love and joy and peace and those kind of things as opposed to a God that lives in the church building or the temple or someone that's in the clouds.'

So much for Joseph, the aggressive capitalist turned Hindu sadhu. Let us postpone our assessment of his experience and reflections until we have heard Ruth's story.

I met her in a forest monastery in a remote corner of Thailand, a radiantly beautiful young woman of thirty-one, with the shaven head and simple white robe of a Buddhist nun. She had grown up in Colorado, and had won a four-year college scholarship with which she prepared herself for social work. She and her family were staunch Lutherans, and attended church every Sunday. But during her university years she took a lot of comparative religion courses with the result that she no longer knew what to believe. Like all her friends, she got turned on to marijuana, and shortly after university, while travelling with a girlfriend in Morocco, tried a few acid trips, LSD. She noticed that when she smoked weed she felt good, felt high, and felt quite open to many things. About this time she happened on Ram Dass's book *Be Here Now* and thought, 'Aha, maybe meditation experiences can lead to something more lasting than just a few hours' high.'

Nixon cut back welfare funds in favour of defence about this time and there were no jobs available in social work, for which she had been trained. So in 1971 she decided to head for India. During her travels in India she noticed the difference between two groups of westerners there: the meditators on the one hand, and on the other hand the drug people, interested only in the cheap drugs they could find. She felt uncomfortable with the drug people. Their lives seemed so empty. She was drawn to the meditators and so she did a ten-day course there with Goenka, a lay Buddhist teacher. Among the meditators she met an Englishman named Andrew who was to become her husband.

The two of them were drawn to the quiet, out-of-the-way places in India, in Nepal, in Thailand, and finally in Laos, where they lived happily in a small rural village for two years, until in 1975 the communists told all the foreigners to leave. This simple life of this village struck Ruth as almost ideal, and she was sad when she and Andrew had to leave. After a little exploration, they found their way to a remote corner of Thailand, near Laos, where they both decided independently 'to ordain', as the Buddhist expression goes, he as a monk and she as a nun. That was where I met her, bright, content, and good-humoured. 'And even though we've lived apart for two and a half years, it's almost like we're more together now than when we lived physically together.'

There were two qualities of life which Ruth said she found in the Laotian village and in this remote Thai monastery near the Laotian border, two things which she had not found where she grew up in the United States. The first was simplicity and naturalness. One of her first experiences in Asia right after college was the ten-day Goenka meditation course already mentioned. It was the simplicity of this Buddhist meditation course, free of any complicated ritual, which drew her. During the two years in Laos and the two and a half years in the forest monastery, her whole life had become enormously simplified, and she contrasted it with the complexity, acquisitiveness and frenetic pace of life back home. She delighted in carrying her own water and having fresh food from the garden or market every day. People grew or made most of what they needed, and had no inclination to make or grow more in order to earn money. 'We felt very comfortable in these countries, especially Laos, where you found your needs were few and you could live happily with not much. I suppose an ordinary American would think of it as poverty level or something of the sort, but actually it was enough to get by.'

Ruth went home for a visit in 1973 after about two years in Asia and found the old life completely empty. She spoke of how depressed she felt when she went to Denver and couldn't see Pike's Peak because of the smog. The little country roads she remembered in the mountains were being replaced by six-lane highways. 'It all seemed so speedy and intense, so removed from nature—buying prepackaged food at the supermarkets, and being out of touch with life and death. In America everything was incredibly speedy, but in Asia people aren't hurried. They have time to *live*. And our speed makes us impersonal, whereas in Asia you get a very personal attitude with people because they're not in a rush. So in the West there's not only the money complexity, but the time and speed of things that are happening and the amount of things you want to get done in one day.

'In the villages in Laos,' she said, 'birth was an exciting thing. Everyone would come and help and see. Death was an exciting thing. People would come and and watch a person die. Even grandchildren would watch the grandfather die. They knew the facts of life quite openly. Nothing was hidden.'

Back in Colorado she found that all her old friends were married and caught up with buying stereos and colour TVs. And she could find no way of communicating to them what her experience in Asia had been.

Simplicity and naturalness, then, growing out of less acquisitiveness and less need of money, a slower and less intense pace of life along with a closeness to all the rhythms of nature—this was, first of all, what Ruth did not find where she grew up, but did find in rural Asia.

Secondly, she spoke of a closer sense of community, a greater social intimacy, a less private and individualistic way of people living together. 'One of the main things which I really enjoy in Asia is you're not isolationists. I mean, you live next door to someone and your really know them; usually you know everything about them. Even in the very friendly Colorado suburb where I lived we rarely knew our next door neighbours. But in Asia, whatever it is, good or bad, people know about it. But it's OK, because it's accepted within the village. You're not isolated. You're in a group. Besides, in the extended family culture of the Laotian village, great respect is shown by everyone, even young people, towards the old people, the senior members of the village. I think that in the States, because of the high value set on individuality, everyone is something special and you have your own little life and it's so important. So I think that in the States you really don't have the time to get involved with anyone else's story because you've got your job, your family, your kids, and you think that if you get involved with other people, they'll take your time, probably your money too. So I suppose people just want to keep to themselves.'

She laughed as she recalled her experience in the church community in which she had grown up: 'Everyone was very loving once a week, every Sunday morning. And then everyone would go to their individual homes some distance away. Maybe a social gathering once a week. Apart from that nobody could care less.'

Ruth loved the harmony of the village. When one person had to build a house, everyone came and helped and it was an occasion where people had a lot of fun. The house was up in two or three days. They helped each other. They shared their rice. And so she and Andrew felt very comfortable there. She mused that back in her Colorado suburb nobody would help build someone a home unless they were their relatives, or were paid. At the end of her college years she and some friends, about five of them, had lived collectively on forty rural acres. But there were always problems. Some would work; some wouldn't. Her friends had also tried several other commune efforts, but they all broke up. 'Why can't people get together?'

When she began to reflect on life in the States, she saw the root of the suffering, the unhappiness, the depression she experienced there as a contrast to what she now experienced as a Buddhist nun. She spoke of the failure to start with oneself and to look at one's own mind. 'People are unaware of the attachment, the clinging which is causing their suffering. It's such a surface kind of life, and your happiness comes from outside instead of from inside. . . . But it's very difficult to help people. Perhaps the only way you can really teach people and help people is by example. So I have to look at myself first.'

Did she plan to return to the States? She answered that in the last few years she had no desire to return even for a visit, but just last month she'd read Stephen Gaskin's book of *Sunday Morning Sermons on the Farm*. The life and philosophy of this Tennessee community of 1,000 people called simply 'The Farm' were very attractive to her. The Farm is a collective which, though not labelled Christian, Buddhist, or anything else, has a strong spiritual basis. They are not just turned in on themselves, not just feeding themselves, but sending food to Guatemala and other places through their PLENTY programme. She was touched that they were not just running away from an evil world in order to escape, but living with the purpose of being helpful to others in very concrete and practical ways.

At the end she summed up, with a smile, the ideal of her own life: 'I feel I'd like to *live*, but in a very free way without wanting anything. But to *live* and to share, and perhaps do something fruitful along the way.'

Now that we have presented a fairly detailed account of Joseph and Ruth, the question naturally arises: 'How typical are they of the seventy people we interviewed?' A rough but honest answer would be: 'Fairly typical.'

Most of the Americans we interviewed were in their twenties or, like Ruth and Joseph, in their early thirties. A few were in their forties or fifties. The younger ones were mostly on some kind of personal search, usually with strong spiritual dimensions. In religious background they were practically all ex-Jews, ex-Catholics, or ex-Protestants. The majority had found the religion of their early years empty rote and ritual for them; a few of them had found it heavy or oppressive. Almost without exception they had at some time experimented with psychedelic drugs, usually escalating from marijuana to LSD or peyote. And also almost without exception they looked back on this drug experience as useful. It helped them to realise, they said, that there were other ways of looking at reality besides the conventional outlook of the culture that surrounded them.

The older people, the minority of those we interviewed, were mostly engaged in some kind of service or business—such occupations as Protestant medical missionaries, Catholic priest teachers of social workers, embassy people, travel agents. These older people generally thought of themselves as having come to give something rather than in search of something. But a number of them, particularly the religious ones, found that they received as much as they gave. Ron, a forty-seven year old Jesuit teacher, had no desire to return to the States. 'There's too much of everything, and the rat-race makes prayer difficult. In the States, I'd probably be a mediocre Jesuit or I'd leave the order.'

The one American trait which earned most praise from these exiles in Asia was energy and drive. But that praise was usually accompanied by the recognition that this drive itself is the source of many of our problems. It easily leads to competitiveness, neurotic compulsion to achievement, and too much of everything.

What they were principally critical of was not so much American religion itself, but the overall culture in the States, a pervasive set of values and attitudes imbedded in the social and economic structures of a technologically advanced capitalist society. Religion was seen as just one epiphenomenon of the general culture; carried by it, not independent of it or shaping it. Indeed, it was the failure of religion to have a significant impact on daily life which led most of the people we interviewed—including those Catholic and Protestant who were part of the 'institutional Church'—to label American mainline religion hypocritical; something to be professed at church on Sunday, but ineffective for the rest of the week.

The qualities whose absence was most lamented by these Americans looking back at their own country from Asia were a contemplative and selfless spirit. Instead of a contemplative spirit, which can relish the present moment for itself, and prize being above doing, they see a busy pragmatic spirit, which values everything primarily as a means to something else. Instead of selflessness and concern for the good of the community, whether large or small, they see an aggressive individualism which ends up isolating people in their loneliness.

I guess you could say that what they would like to see in the States is not new religions, but a transformation of the United States culture as a whole.

Christopher O Donnell

Neo-Pentecostalism in
North America and Europe

AN IMPORTANT revitalisation movement has appeared in the mainline churches since the 1950s and it is designated by a variety of names in different milieux: e.g. (Neo) Pentecostalism, Charismatic Renewal, De Charismatische Vernieuwing, Le Renouveau Spirituel, Charismatischer Aufbruch, Erneuerung, Rinnovamento nell Spirito. The titles themselves indicate differing nuances, but all are unsatisfactory in so far as they fail to specify what is characteristic of the movement. To describe and evaluate the movement presents considerable difficulty, firstly because it is spread throughout the world (as of January 1982 it had Catholic adherents in 110 countries), and secondly, because one can discern different stages of maturity in a particular country, indeed often in a single city. Almost any statement about the movement, which for convenience we will call by its most common English name, Charismatic Renewal, (CR), can be rejected by some group, community or even country as not really reflecting their situation.

The CR is now broadly accepted by the main churches.[1] The welcome by Catholic leaders for CR is quite striking, especially by two popes, Paul VI and John Paul II as well as episcopal conferences. Protestant reception is not uniform: the more fundamentalist churches in general seem to be less well-disposed, whilst the main churches are a good deal more open. One encounters, too, a certain distrust in many Protestant quarters which probably reflects a fear of sectism or schism.

Religious leaders and theologians[2] who observe CR are usually impressed by the serious commitment of its members and by their prayer life. They note with favour the new role given to the experimental dimension of Christian living. Nonetheless, there are serious questions to be faced by CR. The writer raises them from within the movement and in general from a theological perspective with chief emphasis on the Catholic Church though the findings are broadly applicable to other churches as well. The main focus of investigation is the phenomenon of CR in prayer groups and communities. The experience and values of these groups is reflected in CR journals[3] which in their own turn influence these groups and communities. There are also many semi-public newsletters[4] circulating both among the leaders and among a wider public. Furthermore, there is a vast reservoir of material in many thousand tapes which likewise reflects and influences the life of CR. Most aspects of CR have been examined by competent theologians. From the Catholic side the prestigious Malines Documents

35

sponsored and mostly authored by Cardinal Suenens are particularly important as well as the forthcoming article, 'Pentecôtisme' in the *Dictionnaire de Spiritualité* by Francis A. Sullivan which will be definitive for some time. Articles on the movement have appeared in many theological and pastoral journals over the past decade,[5] and the movement has been extensively studied by sociologists and psychologists.[6]

1. MEMBERSHIP OF CHARISMATIC RENEWAL

It has been observed that the appearance of CR in the Catholic Church took unawares not only theologians and the hierarchy but above all the social scientists. These last were surprised not only because of their previous perception of the Catholic Church but also because of existing studies of Classical Pentecostalism whose members were largely seen to be drawn from the more disadvantaged and black population in the US. The CR on the other hand attracted mainly an educated middle class which was remarkably open to the emotional dimensions of religious involvement rather than to the merely intellectual. Moreover, the early growth in US of CR was in a technological, rationalist culture and in a Church which had stressed as high values order and institutions.

The mainly, but not by any means exclusively, middle-class profile of CR adherents is observable primarily in Europe and the United States. The failure in these continents to attract lower social classes on a wide scale is probably the result of several factors. One could point to Pentecostal language and idiom which is alien to cradle Catholics, to the structure of meetings whose major emphasis on hymns and Scripture reading may repel the functionally (semi) illiterate, and to other features of the CR such as conferences, day-meetings that involve travel and other expenses.

Women predominate at all charismatic functions, though they do not have leadership roles commensurate with their numbers, professional training or educational levels. The single largest vocational grouping is religious sisters whose numbers at CR exceed the societal percentage.

Membership is difficult to assess. The normal designation within CR is 'to be involved'. This can cover a very wide range of commitment. It respects the fact that like Alcoholics Anonymous (with which CR has many structural and organisational similarities)[7] there is no formal admission, registration or expulsion. The penetration of CR in the Church is hard to gauge. A Gallup poll in the US (1980) gave as 18 per cent the percentage of Catholics who consider themselves as charismatic or Pentecostal and one-sixth of this number pray in tongues. This last gives some indication of fuller commitment.

Recruitment to the movement does not follow uniform patterns. Though there are some who find it accidentally, there is evidence to indicate that people are more likely to become involved through face-to-face encounters with friends, relatives or fellow members of the same job, association or group. The initial approach to CR can often be the result of some strong persuasion or encouragement by others, but pressure is not sufficient to keep people attending.

There has been much analysis of reasons why people are attracted by CR. Sociologists and psychologists have indicated some facilitative or conditioning factors in people's inclination towards CR. These include disillusionment at the failure to implement the reforms of Vatican II, insecurity as a result of changes since the Council. Clergy and religious who find themselves in conflict-situations *vis-à-vis* the institutional Church and those who feel little sense of belonging in urban parishes can experience a sense of real or perceived alienation from God or from the institutional Church and lack personal or ideological 'wholeness', so that there is a need for meaning, healing and conversion. The value of such indicators is limited; there is no homogeneity in the CR and they probably reflect the majority of the Catholic population which remains outside the movement.

As yet there is no consistent picture of growth/decline in the CR. The enthusiasm of the early 1970s has clearly waned and the numbers attending mass conferences has dropped, at times dramatically. The cost of attending expensively mounted events in recessionary and inflationary times is clearly a contributory factor. There is also a very large number of 'lapsed charismatics' and of those who are not as involved as formerly. In the absence of adequate studies one can only suggest tentative reasons: some find the challenge of moving from early enthusiasm to regular commitment too demanding; some fail to integrate CR into the rest of their lives and so find its meaning for them deficient; some experience tension between involvement in CR and other commitments such as marriage, religious life, career. Though there is a fall-off in places, elsewhere there is growth.

Another phenomenon is the splintering of groups. The reason is rarely because a group was found to be too big; it is usually in order to establish the CR in another place. The results are ambiguous: there is dilution as the movement expands into a new area from a larger group and there is a dispersal of talents and gifts, both the charismatic as well as the social and organisational ones.

2. MAJOR ISSUES

Under the headline of major issues one can consider key strengths and weaknesses of CR as a renewal movement. They are areas critical for the health of the CR and need further study by scholars of various disciplines as well as care by those in pastoral positions.

(a) Baptism in the Holy Spirit and Charisms

The key impact of CR is clearly the conversion experience with openness to the gifts of the Holy Spirit which is usually called 'Baptism in the Holy Spirit', though many are unhappy with this term. A new opening to the experiential in religion normally follows. In the CR there is usually careful preparation called Life in the Spirit Seminar before prayer for this outpouring of the Holy Spirit. This preliminary seminar is strongly evangelistic and centres on bringing people to a new acceptance of Jesus as Lord and Saviour.

An expectation of gifts of the Spirit is an identifying trait of CR which distinguishes it from other revivalist or conversion movements. The spirituality of the CR, however, is not so much pneumatological as Christological: if it risks any distortion it is being Jesus-centred rather than fully trinitarian.

Major studies on the properly charismatic dimension of CR continue to appear.[8] But the gifts risk being marginalised away from the centre of the Church's life which would be a negation of *Lumen gentium* §12. Some specific points might be made about the various gifts.

Healing is not always curing—many are 'healed' in Lourdes but not 'cured'. Though distortions are still found and one encounters harmful expectations of widespread cures, there is now a better understanding of healing within the context of redemptive suffering. More dialogue with the medical profession, especially with psychiatrists, is needed in the whole area of healing.

Deliverance often reflects an excessively dualist view of the world. The CR has a valid insight into the role of Satan, but the focus is often distorted. In the fifth Malines Document on The Power of Darkness and the Charismatic Renewal, Cardinal Suenens sharply corrects deviations and proposes a pastoral strategy within a wide theological perspective.

Prophecy has been inadequately studied as a charism, though its role has been noted by sociologists. A major source for much-needed investigation will be the mystical doctors even though they might seem, at first sight, to give a negative judgment on the advisability or even admissability of this charism.

(b) Community

Community is one of the most important fruits of the CR. In the early 1970s the enormously talented leaders at Ann Arbor saw it as their main task to develop their own community called 'The World of God' and to foster the growth of charismatic communities world-wide. They did this with characteristic commitment. Within a few years there was an international fellowship of several dozen communities. Moreover, the CR world-wide was alerted to the need to develop communities if prayer groups were not to remain at the level of spiritual service stations. The fruits of these communities are to be found in deepened commitment in all areas of life and in the rediscovery of important New Testament values.

A weakness of the Word of God Community approach is an insistence on uniformity based on one particular reading of the Scriptures. The role of women is a clear instance: they cannot be leaders and the model allowed for marriage is largely that of the head/submissive wife (see Eph. 5.22-23). Reasons other than biblical literalism like the wearing of veils (see I Cor. 11:6) are involved; what appears to the writer to be a down-grading of women is a deliberate attempt to establish a proper *male* role in the family and community.

Charismatic communities are necessarily élitist in some sense. The very demanding obligations of meetings, prayer, sharing-time will exclude those whose family or work situation, spiritual or psychological maturity do not permit such intense commitment. Not all groups or communities make the quasi-total demands of the Word of God variety: some exist as prayer groups with some heightened awareness of caring for one another.

Religious life might be expected to have something to teach charismatic communities. But it is not very well understood, and CR leaders do not see enough spiritual vitality in religious life to prompt them to look to it for guidance or inspiration. Most spokespersons for the CR see community as a new growth in the Church, comparable in some way with religious life.

(c) Leadership

The exercise of leadership in the CR has received much attention from sociologists who have noted its dynamics, manipulative factors, controls exercised over non-acceptable behaviour, widespread anti-feminism and possible authoritarian-style abuses. Theologians have not studied important ecclesiological issues which arise in CR leadership.

In the Word of God Community (Ann Arbor) and in communities and groups influenced by it, there is a style of leadership which comes from one particular New Testament model. Elders or heads are placed over those who are being 'disciplined' and thus 'in submission'. Elders or pastoral heads exercise a role which reflects some of the functions associated with a confessor, spiritual director or religious superior, but long experience and law have built in some important protections needed by CR communities. This pattern of leadership has many values, especially pragmatic ones of good order, sense of direction, techniques for handling difficult people or situations. The range of the influence of the 'pastoral head' can extend to such matters as job choice, vacations, choice of marriage partner, relationships within marriage and family.

In less structured prayer groups and communities there is not so much directive leadership. The danger present to all CR leadership is that it claims to be charismatic—there is an appeal to the Spirit who is presumed to be directing the leaders. There arises, therefore, a pressure to conform which in extreme cases can resemble spiritual blackmail. There is little genuine dialogue except amongst the leaders themselves. Those outside the leadership group are expected to accept decisions already reached.

Various control techniques are necessary to any organisation. Those who are in conflict with leaders are usually treated with great love and kindness, but compromise is normally excluded as this would take from the charismatic discernment of the leaders. At another level speakers can be 'banned' and various books be unavailable at charismatic outlets. The converse also operates: groups and conferences will invite only those who can be relied upon to endorse the accepted viewpoint.

A further example of the closed circle of authority is the process of selection of leaders. These emerge by a process of discernment in which existing leaders have a major role. Rarely are there obvious means for removing leaders: some argue from Rom. 11:29 that leaders should be permanent.

Ecclesiologically there are major questions which must be raised. The CR is not a lay movement but is composed of clergy, religious and laity. If it fails in its perceived vocation of renewal of the whole Church then its leadership will pose no theological problem—it can be any style compatible with charity and common sense. But if it is to be at the heart of the Church then the leadership will eventually have to reflect the hierarchical structure of the Church and appropriate roles for the bishop, priests and deacons will have to emerge in service of the whole people of God. Otherwise it will remain ecclesiologically marginalised. These implications have not been faced by CR leaders or by the Church authorities.

(d) Theology and the Charismatic Renewal

We have already noted major theological writing on CR and emerging from within the movement, nonetheless, theology within the CR and the attitude of some key leaders of the movement in the US to theology is a crucial weakness. It is not mainly the question of heterodox beliefs noted by some observers. The main areas are a tendency to imminent eschatology (often implicit in calls to conversion) and a false doctrine on assurance of salvation. Beliefs of this kind are not a major problem.

The real issues are much deeper and they emerge mostly, but not exclusively, from the milieu of the influential Word of God Community (Ann Arbor). This community has served the world-wide CR unselfishly and fruitfully. To criticise it is thus distasteful, but unavoidable. The writer finds it necessary to take issue both with the attitude to theology and with the theology espoused in many of the books published by the community as well as in the periodicals *New Covenant* (in aim Roman Catholic, circ. 74,000 monthly) and *Pastoral Renewal* (avowedly interdenominational and directed to those in pastoral leadership, circ. 20,000). Though these are not theological journals, their material suffers from serious isolation from the mainstream of theology. The profound concerns and questioning which preoccupy theologians such as Congar, de Lubac, Metz, Rahner or Van Balthasar—to name but a few Europeans—find little significant echo on their pages. The Ann Arbor leadership is instead more active in

D

attacking enemies of the Christian message who are supporters of historical-critical exegesis, humanism, modern feminism and moral theology which does not follow the clear teaching of the *magisterium*.

The theology emerging from this school and those influenced by it is at times fundamentalist. The theologian is seen merely as a mouthpiece of the *magisterium*. There is little need for creative theology as the truths needed are clear in the Bible and tradition. The value of this approach is great clarity on burning issues such as abortion and divorce. It shows, too, an effective application of scripture to such problems of daily living as diverse as anger, debt or the rearing of children. But there is a very disquieting frequency of the definite article: we are presented with *the* scriptural doctrine rather than with *an* interpretation of the Bible (which might be defective).

There is also a policy of shunning polemics, even to the point of avoiding self-defence; in practice this involves a refusal to enter into meaningful dialogue. The Ann Arbor doctrine or judgment is delivered; if it is not accepted there is a self-protective withdrawal into the mutually confirming and supportive environment. Apart from the obvious danger of a CR ghetto, there is loss also to the Church: statements which are presented in a take-it-or-leave-it fashion may need nuance or modification. Without dialogue useful insights or doctrine may be rejected.

A final question might be raised about the catholicity of *New Covenant*: it does carry articles of special interest to Catholics. But the frequency of writing by Christians of other churches or by professedly 'non-denominational Christians' as well as acute sensitivity to the perspectives of other faiths all leave the magazine open to the charge of lacking a deeply felt Catholic ethos.

(e) Outreach—Service

From the outset CR has been criticised for its apparent lack of commitment to social action. For the sociologist the movement is expressive rather than instrumental, or in other analyses, it is a combination of traditional and promotional models.[9] In theological terms the CR relates to the world in terms of judgment rather than incarnation, especially in the *New Covenant* type of theology, though this is not universal. If the CR were only to be a particular life-style in the Church, then the issue would be less important. It is the self-awareness of the CR as an instrument of renewal for the whole Church that makes its failure in this area so critical.

In many sectors of the CR there has been a deliberate decision to combat the evils of society through personal conversion and community. Evangelisation thus becomes the favoured work of the CR and takes various forms though it rarely attains the depth of *Evangelii nuntiandi*, much less Puebla.

(f) Ecumenism

The CR has been ecumenical from the beginning. It sought the renewal of the Church, a primary ecumenical task (Vatican II, *Ecumenism* §3). It has also been ecumenical in having Christians of various denominations in varied faith-sharing experiences. There is some danger of mere non-denominationalism, a direction severely censured by the second Malines Document. A problem for Catholics is Protestant cultural and theological accretions in various aspects of the life of the movement. The theologians who have written most sensitively on this matter are Cardinal Suenens and Killian McDonnell.

In Britain there is some concern that the house churches (small groups of people of no denomination) are drawing away people from their own denomination. Most of the house churches are Pentecostal to some degree and through them the immature become disaffected with the institutional Church and its sacramental system. Elsewhere the 'come out' phenomenon though widespread is not a major problem.

CONCLUSION

An evaluation of the impact of the CR at this stage must be tentative. It has influenced many aspects of the life of the Church, especially liturgy, and has had a positive effect on millions of Catholics. But it has tended to become marginalised and is now in a trap: it will not be taken seriously by theologians and pastors unless it corrects weaknesses mentioned earlier, but it needs the help of these same theologians and Church leaders to achieve its special calling. Bishops tend to value the evident fruits of the movement rather than the movement itself. Most would see it as just one among the many worthwhile aspects of the life of the diocese. Pope John Paul II seems to have sensed the dilemma of the CR in his address to the International Leaders Conference (1981) when he called on them to take the initiative in building bonds of trust and cooperation with the bishops. The lesson of history is that only those renewals that affect the structures of the Church really persist. Though its most articulate spokespersons and theologians perceive the CR as a movement for the renewal of the whole Church, the 'New Pentecost' of Pope John XXIII's prayer, it still risks remaining a revival and developing yet more sect characteristics. It must find a way of genuine dialogue with the whole Church as well as with the world. It will have to broaden its appeal upwards and downwards on the social scale. It will have to move to the heart of the Church.

It has the vitality to do all these necessary things.

Notes

1. See *Presence, Power and Praise* ed. K. McDonnell, 3 vols (Minnesota 1980), a collection of 104 official statements, to which add German Bishops 'Erneuerung der Kirche aus dem Geist Gottes' (May 1981). Note perceptive analysis by K. McDonnell 'Towards a Critique of the Churches and the Charismatic Renewal' *One in Christ* 16 (1980) 329-337.

2. E.g. from Catholic side, Norbert Baumert, Robert Faricy, Domenico Grasso, René Laurentin, Killian McDonnell, Heribert Mühlen and the exegetes Arnold Bittlinger, Francis Martin, George Martin, George Montague.

3. E.g. *Alleluia* (Italy), *Erneuerung in Kirche und Gesellschaft* (W. Germany), *Goed Nieuws* (Belgium), *Il est vivant!* (France), *Magnificat* (Belgium), *New Covenant* (USA), *New Creation* (Ireland).

4. E.g. *International Newsletter of International Communications Office* (Rome), *De Nieuwe Aarde* (Belgium), *Pecos Benedictine* (USA), *Renewal in the Spirit* (for religious—Rome), *Rundbrief der charismatischen Erneuerung in der katholischen Kirche* (Passau).

5. E.g. *Clergy Review, La Civiltà Cattolica, Concilium, The Furrow, Nouveau Revue Théologique, Review for Religious, Stimmen der Zeit, La Vie spirituelle.*

6. E.g. *Archives de sciences sociales des religions, Journal for the Scientific Study of Religion, Review for Religious Research, Social Compass.* Add *Pro mundi vita* 60 (1976) and note also important studies by André Godin especially *Psychologie des expériences religieuses* (Paris 1981).

7. See I. P. Gellman *The Sober Alcoholic. An Organisational Analysis of Alcoholics Anonymous* (New Haven 1964).

8. Note in particular Francis A. Sullivan *Charisma and the Charismatic Renewal* (Ann Arbor, Dublin 1982).

9. See J. Remy, E. Servais and J. P. Hiernaux as reported by C. Degive *Le Discours Charismatique. Perspectives sociologiques* (Louvain University 1976-77) Annexes II.

Christian Lalive d'Epinay

Political Regimes and Millenarianism in a Dependent Society: Reflections on Pentecostalism in Chile

1. INTRODUCTION

IN AN ARTICLE which appeared some time ago, B. Wilson (1958—see Bibliography) pointed out that in sociology of religion, while one looks to exogenous factors to explain the birth of a religious movement, its continuation and evolution depend on internal factors, not related to society as a whole. This observation is still valid in general terms, even if there are notable exceptions.

I propose to start from the axiom that the dynamic of a part of the social whole should be interpreted in conjunction with the dynamic of that whole. So a sect, however far it tries to push its break with the established order in a society, always remains part of society as a whole. This proposition should of course not be taken either in terms of classical functionalism nor, still less, in those of behaviourism.

The question is not one of the sect being a functioning part of a dependent capitalist society, if we are dealing with the case of Chile. It does of course fulfil a function, or rather several functions. But here the aim is to treat a religious group as a social agent, situated in a particular socio-cultural setting. Modifications of this setting then change the possibilities for action on the part of this religious group. These changes do not constitute a stimulus automatically producing a definite adaptive response; the agent receives the changes as signals which he analyses in relation to his cultural system, and these signals contribute to the modification of his field of possible actions. To the extent that a religious movement constitutes a complex agent in itself, this modification from outside can also modify the balance of its relationship of internal forces, the relationship between the different groups that make it up. So, faced with evolution in society as a whole, the agent acts as a '*structuring mediation*'.

For his part, the sociologist may try to unravel the '*field of possibilities*' facing each agent in a given spatio-temporal context; he will then be able to classify the various responses open to the agent according to the degree of possibility that each will come about. But it will still be the case that a given agent, in a given context, can always opt for the least probable course (on this point, see Lalive d'Epinay, 1974). Throughout the

42

course of my studies of Protestant minorities in Latin America, I have always tried to indicate the different possible dynamics of different religious types, taking account both of the structural elements of the type under consideration and the specific characteristics of dependent capitalist societies of the sub-continent (see Lalive d'Epinay, 1975, chs. 6 and 7).

Here I should like to sum up the results of earlier studies on Pentecostalism in Chile (in particular, 1972). From 1965 to the present, three Presidents, each putting forward very differing ideologies and development plans, each based on different forces in the country, have followed one another in Chile. The first two came to power as a result of elections taking place within the framework of the Constitution, the third as the result of a *coup d'état*. First came the reformist government of President Eduardo Frei, Christian Democrat (1965-1970), then President Allende with his Popular Front government aiming to transform society in a socialist direction (1970-1973), and finally the military, reactionary government of General Pinochet, aiming to purify Chile and restore Christian—and capitalist—civilisation.

In the context of this article, the question I should like to examine is the political inclinations and orientations of the Pentecostal movement, and in particular how the political evolution of Chile has influenced the general thrust of this religious movement. But before going on to this central theme, it will be as well to look at certain elements in the genesis of the Pentecostal movement in Chile and certain aspects of its social make-up and its ideological system.

2. THE STRUCTURAL CRISIS AND THE IMPLANTATION OF PENTECOSTALISM

(a) The structural crisis of Chile in the 'neo-imperialist' period

The establishment of Pentecostalism in Chile is closely related to the transition from the 'imperialist period' to the 'neo-imperialist' one, that is to the crisis of the 1930s (known as the Great Crisis). As far as the internal affairs of Chile are concerned, all the literature stresses the decisive character of the years 1920-1935: exhaustion of reclaimable land under the *hacienda* (estate) system, the nitrate crisis, the end of 'outward growth', inflation, the beginning of massive internal migration. . . .

On the political and ideological plane, it was in these decades that the revolutionary project ceased to belong to the domain of Utopia and became translated into organisations and actions, mostly of the working classes but also of the lower ranks of the middle classes. The first President Alessandri carried out a demagogic policy, increasing employment in the public sector so as to mop up at least part of the discontent. The 1930s were of course a period of unstable government. The return to 'legality'—that great Chilean myth—took place in 1932, with Alessandri's resumption of the Presidency. But the dominated rural classes remained on the fringes of this process, which affected them through internal migrations and the decline of the ideology of the *patrón*.

Reading Chilean history from 1930 to 1970 outside the general context of the world capitalist system gives the impression of a society whose structures have broken down looking for a new equilibrium. But this is an optical illusion: once Chile is placed in the context of the world situation, this period is seen not to be one of transition, so not to comprise an *anomie* (a breaking-down of old rules and a search for new ones). The Chilean crisis has a structure, but its principle (or structural nexus) lies outside the country itself: seen in the context of the world capitalist system, the *permanent crisis* of Chile becomes understandable since it takes on an ordering principle. Whence the concept of *structured crisis* in the sense of an (exogenous) structuring of a crisis situation in a dependent body.

In an infrastructural framework like this, everything favours the growth of salvationist ideologies. But they have to be there in the first place. In other words, the conditions necessary for the growth of new redemptorist ideologies come together, but these conditions are not enough in themselves to ensure their expansion. But once these ideologies are present, they will spread:

(i) among the social classes most affected by the crisis, and
(ii) within these, among those classes least effectively touched by directly political ideologies.

(b) A short history of Pentecostalism

It started in the United States at the beginning of this century. *Theologically*, it insists on the gifts of the Spirit (baptism of fire, glossolalia, sacred dance, gift of healing, gift of evangelising). *Sociologically*, it reintroduces the 'rites of possession' into Christianity, and so a whole new language and new mode of communication with other people and with the sacred, radically different from those of the great churches. It has a mode of expression which, as we shall see, has some analogies with that of the dominated classes.

It influenced a group of Methodists who were 'into' mystical research. This group was excluded from the Methodist Church in Chile (which was then a 'colonial' type of church) in the years 1909-1910. There was only one *gringo* (foreigner) among those excluded. Cut off from foreign missionaries and their dollar funds, this group from the start took on a national character and either had to grow or die out. Till 1930, its growth was slow, and came mainly from bringing about a number of schisms in the Protestant churches. So growth was more through transferring believers from one body to another than through non-believers changing into believers.

From 1930 to 1960, growth was explosive. The cumulative annual total of Protestant growth remained practically stable during these three decades: between 6 and 7 per cent. This meant that the number of *evangélicos* doubled every ten or eleven years, till it was nearly half a million in 1960 (5·6 per cent of the population).[1] Then, from 1960 to 1970, this tide started running out and the Protestant growth rate was only slightly higher than the natural growth of the population as a whole.

(c) Pentecostalism and social class

While it is clear that Pentecostalism has become a religious expression of the dominated classes, the question of the exact relationship between this millenarianism and the different sub-classes and strata within the dominated classes still cannot be exactly determined. An examination of this question has recently been published in *Social Compass* (1978, Vol. XXV/1, by J. Tennekes and myself). Here I should like just to summarise some of our conclusions.

Pentecostalism is particularly widespread among those members of the dominated classes without stable employment: the urban sub-proletariat, the rural proletariat and semi-proletariat, the lower ranks of the middle classes. This analysis in terms of social class can help to show why, while they both grow in the same overall social terrain, Marxism and Pentecostalism engage in a sort of 'general post' rather than in real competition. Marxist ideology (in both its communist and socialist versions) spreads traditionally *from the place of work*. Pentecostalism, on the other hand, spreads *from the home*. Till the time of the second President Alessandri (till the 1960s, that is), trades unions among the peasants were illegal. In practice, the spread of unions among rural workers dates only from the period of Christian Democracy.

This helps to explain the juxtaposition between a secular ideology which calls for the re-structuring of human society and a sacred ideology which proclaims the coming of the kingdom of God: starting from the home, Pentecostalism sees its effectiveness diminish the closer it comes to groups in stable employment; used to being based on the place of work, Marxism languishes among the 'marginals', particularly as it was forbidden access to the *fundos* (estates), real ecological fortresses, till the recent Allende years.

In effect, Pentecostalism was the only 'possession' of the dominated rural population from 1930 to about 1967: other ideologies obviously belonging to the *patrón*—including that of the priest who came to celebrate mass in the *hacienda* chapel!

3. THE STRUCTURE OF PENTECOSTAL COMMUNITIES

(a) Idealised reconstruction of traditional social structure

'Traditional' here designates the oldest social sectors. The millenarianist community restored the ideological image of the social structure of the *hacienda*, reinterpreted (and so idealised, distorted, not the reality the image claims to reflect), just when this ideological image was beginning to suffer from a very serious 'credibility gap'. The ideology of the *hacienda* has been described as being based on three beliefs: the value of face-to-face relationships; the conviction that the boss will always be there to sort out difficulties; and the '*mito del patroncito*', the conviction that the owner holds his power from an age-old tradition going back finally to God, '*pues siempre ha sido así, y así debe ser*' ('since it's always been that way, and that's the way it has to be') (Medina, 1964).

Now, the Pentecostal community is based on face-to-face relationships[2]; it is a truly fraternal community which resolves specific problems (it assigns rights and duties—so human dignity—to its members, and sets up a system of mutual help under the aegis of the pastor); finally, the pastor takes up the role of the *patrón* in that he, too, acts in an authoritarian manner (he usually appoints his deputies, and if a vote is taken—which is rare—it is only to ratify the decision he has already taken). If he behaves like this, it is because he is God's chosen one, and has proved as much by founding the Church (or, if he is only a successor, by making it grow). The pastor has all the rights, because he is God's *lieu-tenant*, he holds God's place. His power comes from God, as he has proved by 'opening up the ways of the Lord'. And so the '*mito del patroncito*' is re-embodied in what might be termed a '*mito del pastorcito*'.

But there is also a break with the traditional social structure: the Pentecostal assembly can be compared to a people's army; it is full of different ranks, but these are not based on social class. Everyone (except women!) can reach the top of the ladder 'if he has the gift'—in secular terms, if he proves to be a 'natural leader'. I have known men converted at fifty to begin as *obreros* (labourers) at sixty, this being the first pastoral grade, the term alluding to the 'labourers in the vineyard of the Lord'. Within a rigidly stratified society, where upward mobility can only be from one generation to the next, Pentecostalism provides the opportunity for new forms of mobility: 'The sect substitutes religious status for social status' (M. Pope).

But—the final point to stress, and again analogous with the *hacienda*—the Pentecostal assembly is a *totalitarian society* which requires the individual to give himself over totally to it, abandoning his own free will for the sake of the group.

The underlying aim of this movement is to cut itself off completely from 'the world' (synonymous with the principle of evil) and to become a social Utopia. Two things prevent it from doing this:

(i) The very definition of *work* in a Pentecostal sense, which is to challenge the world (crusade) so as to call it to repentance and proclaim the imminence of the judgment and the kingdom (an apocalyptic call much helped by Chile's frequent earthquakes!).

(ii) The fact that the movement has never tried (at least in South America) to form an ecological community, living and even working together—for lack of a suitable model, perhaps? Pentecostalism exerts its influence entirely on the *free time* of its faithful, but they have to go into the 'world' to earn their living.

These two reasons cause the *basic contradiction* in Pentecostalism: it preaches a break with the world, but has to live alongside it, work in it and even use it as a source for its proselytes. In an attempt to resove this contradiction, it teaches an ethic of passivity in their lives outside the community: *'no te metas'* ('don't get involved').

Pentecostalism as a social structure can be summed up in three '-isms': authoritarianism (pastoral paternalism), totalitarianism and egalitarianism. We now need to enquire into its representational system.

(b) Pentecostalist ideology: a pre-millenarianist dualism with totalitarian claims

(i) The axes of pre-millenarianist dualism

An impressive print often forms the chief ornament in Pentecostal churches. It shows a raging sea whose waves beat against a rocky isle. A Bible rests on this threatened spot of land, its pages open, lit by a ray of light from heaven, shooting through the black storm clouds; on the pages of the Bible, this verse, or a similar one, appears in large letters: 'Come to me, all you who labour and are overburdened, and I will give you rest' (Matt. 11:28). This picture[3] gives an allegorical representation of some of the principle tenets of Pentecostalist ideology. In a world of perdition and misery, radically 'evil and perverse', there are little islands of peace, the communities of believers protected by the 'power of God',[4] the Spirit who comes from on high. The task of the faithful is to help those who are drowning, to call them on to the sheltered shores of the Church, but without thinking of trying to calm the troubled waters themselves.

This cosmology rests on a deep dualism which expects everything from the spiritual realm and nothing from the material. This picture does not illustrate the waiting theme; this is, nevertheless, a basic element in this dualism. The community, the refuge of the converted placed under the protection of the Consoler, is sustained by its waiting for a kingdom whose imminence it proclaims, and of which the Church is not the earnest but only the sign. The coming of the kingdom will mean the destruction of all that is and the building of a new heaven and a new earth.

The cosmology of sectarian Protestantism implies a religious view of society as well: the dualist paradigm spirit/matter, expressed on the cosmological plane by that of heavens/world, goes on to produce the antithesis church/society. Since this world is condemned, why bother with it? But how far can this ethic of abstention which governs the believer's ethic be taken? Here the cosmological framework leaves a certain margin of choice and behaviour open to the socio-political activity of believers. Will this show itself in active strikes, challenging human laws, demonstrating through confrontation that its followers have already left this world to enter another with no common denominator with this one? Or will it rather show in systematic passivity, a policy of abstention wherever human laws authorise this?

It is in fact this second type of socio-political behaviour that is in evidence, what we might call *conformist passivity*. Pre-millenarianist waiting engenders a detachment from the world that does not easily show itself in conflict. The commandment, 'do not love the world and the things of the world' from the first Letter of St John (much quoted in these religious movements) is tempered by the injunction of obedience to the civil authorities laid by St Paul on the Christians of Rome (Rom. 13:1-7). The politics of Pentecostalists is based on *their view of the relationship* between these two biblical references. This legitimises what the law lays down as obligatory, accepts a certain degree of participation in the world, but condemns all *responsible* participation. Whence the general proscription of all political commitment, which by definition cannot be a passive act.

To sum up: the axes of Pentecostalist ideology are sythesised in the basic paradigm:

spiritual   *versus*   material

which can be permutated into the following series:

spirit	*versus*	body
believer	,,	'gentile' (non-believer)
heavens	,,	earth
transcendent	,,	immanent
Church	,,	world
kingdom	,,	society
God	,,	Devil
Good	,,	Evil

And this ideology is linked to a strategy for action that combines the law of submission to the authorities (the State) and that of breaking with the world, of detachment.

(ii) *The totalitarian claim in practice*

Without going too deeply into the matter, it should be stressed that the ideology and the social system mutually support one another to make the totalitarian claim real and effective and to impose the breaking-off from the world on the faithful.

Let us take the case of a believer who accepts the post of a trades union official:

—he will have less time for his church, which claims a monopoly on his free time. The pastor will begin to mutter: '*Está en cosas del mundo, se pierde . . .*' ('He's involved in the affairs of the world. He's lost . . .')

—in the union, the believer learns another form of participation, based not on giving in to authority, but on exchange of views, on discussion. When his pastor seeks to warn him, he will try to discuss the matter. (Once, trying to organise a debate with a group of Pentecostal leaders, I said, 'We might discuss this among ourselves . . .', and the pastor told me: 'Not discuss, brother. Converse . . .'). His reply will be interpreted as a challenge to the very power principle (whose source is sacred) in the community. Excommunication will follow, justified by referring to the need to choose between God and Mammon.

(iii) *The conservative role of Pentecostalism in society*

The reader must by now have been reminded of Marx's dictum that religion is the opium of the people. But one needs to look at the whole paragraph of which the phrase 'opium of the people' is the conclusion:

Religion is, on the one hand, the *expression* of real poverty, and, on the other, *protestation* against real poverty. It is the sigh of the creature bowed down, the feeling of a world without heart, as it is the spirit of an age deprived of spirit. It is the opium of the people.

(Marx, 1844. The italics are Marx's own.)

Clearly, in a dependent capitalist society, Pentecostalism supports the established order through its passivity and submission. But it also offers a dangerous alternative to it, because it offers the dominated classes a *coherent, complete and effective ideological response* to their situation: for the rural dominated classes in Chile, between 1920 and 1960, there was no real alternative other than revolution or acceptance. The danger of Pentecostalism is that, like all *ideologies*, it fulfils the role of legitimising a system of actions: in this case it legitimises passivity. And since it is a religious ideology, it legitimises it through recourse to the *sacred*, which has always been the most effective source of legitimacy. So, following Paulo Freire, one can say that the danger of Pentecostalism comes from the fact that it forms the 'oppressed consciousness'; it sets it in a cosmology, and so hardens it. Does this not make all mobilisation virtually impossible?

But while recognising this fact, let us not lose sight of the fact that, as analysis of the situation of the rural poor and those on the fringe of the cities till the 1960s shows, Pentecostalism was in fact the *only* coherent ideological stance they could possibly take. While it may alienate man from society, we must allow it to give its followers a minimum of human dignity, which society had taken from them.[5]

4. POLITICAL REGIMES AND RELIGIOUS DYNAMICS

Our analysis of the structure of Pentecostalism has led us to demonstrate the rule of *conformist passivity* which governs the relationships between the religious minority and society as a whole. This rule will now enable us to evaluate the modes of Pentecostal reaction to political change.

(a) The 'reformist-participationist' political regime and the stabilisation of Pentecostalism (1965-1970)

The Christian Democrat programme was carried out against a background of the theory of modernisation and of structural dualism. In it, the existence of large marginal sectors of society is the expression of the survival of traditional society alongside modern society. The national development plan required the 'marginals' to be incorporated into the national market, that they become both wage-earners and consumers. One of the main thrusts of the Christian Democrat programme was to try to mobilise these sectors of the population and press them into organising themselves, and so participating. Neighbourhood associations, fathers' groups, mothers' groups, peasant trades unions, all sorts of voluntary associations flourished under President Frei. The philosophical basis of the movement was borrowed from the Christian Personalism of Edouard Mounnier; its socio-economic aim was the creation of an enlarged national market; many, of course, saw this as a basis for electoral manipulation.

At the same time, the Catholic Church was carrying out a deep pastoral reform—partly influenced by its reflection on the numerical growth of sects—aimed at adopting a strategy designed to increase the numbers of 'base communities'. So suddenly, after 1965, Pentecostalism, which had been the only movement operating among the 'popular classes' (rural poor, urban fringe) till then, found itself faced with growing competition.

These new voluntary associations taught a new form of participation which opposed the communitary ideal to that of sectarian totalitarianism. While reflection and discussion may sometimes have tipped over into demagogy, there was a stress on the idea of personal responsibility, a call to all to commit themselves. The point of departure—the actual conditions of life—remained the same, but these communities called on their members to recognise these consciously and to work out responses stemming from them. So the rural poor received one set of messages, with one set of suggested solutions, the urban poor another.

It would seem that the more real possibilities of direct participation Latin American societies offer their 'dominated classes', the greater will be the tension between belonging to the Pentecostal movement on one hand, and consciousness of being a citizen of the country and a member of a social class heavy with historical possibility on the other (see Lalive d'Epinay, 1969, p. 172). But does this suggest that there will be a decline in numbers for Pentecostalism, or that it will change, undergoing a qualitative transformation of its social structure? One has to be careful here, because the effects on sectarian Protestantism are largely dependent on an unstable overall situation.

Let us take two possible cases:

(i) in countries where Pentecostalism has only recently taken root, it is likely that it will decline in numbers;

(ii) where it is deeply entrenched, as it is in Chile, where it is now a major constitutive element of the popular classes and their culture, its decline is only likely over a very long term. A tradition has been formed, which already goes back three generations.

In 1972 I noted that it was unlikely that the Census figures from 1970, when published, would show any fall-off in the rate of growth of Pentecostalism. In fact, as has been seen, the rate of growth was low between 1965 and 1970. The competition from new forms of popular mobilisation seems to have had an immediate effect on Pentecostalist expansion.

If this particular political regime had stayed in power for a long period, what might have happened?

If the growing opportunities for participatory action offered by society had been accompanied by a slowing of the growth rate of Pentecostalism, then a qualitative change would have followed, in the direction of the type of 'Protestantism of sanctification' (or 'denomination'). Pre-millenarianist sects, based on the hope of the Kingdom, find it hard to withstand the passage of time! The Kingdom is a long time coming, and they have to settle into the provisional period, which grows longer. Only a process of continuous expansion, the constant arrival of converts who are only just beginning their wait for the Kingdom, can keep their apocalyptic hope alive.

All over Latin America, it is still the case that Pentecostalism is growing at such a rate that the spirit and fervour of the 'first generation' are handed on intact. But when those who are 'born in the spirit' (as their language has it) begin to outnumber the 'converts', and when furthermore the sacred work of the community loses its meaning because it is no longer effective, then change is inevitable.

(b) A society in transition: the possible change in Pentecostalism (1970-1973)

The coming to power of the Government of Popular Unity under Dr Allende in 1970 created a new situation. Here was a regime which did not merely practise a populist policy towards the dominated classes, but which claimed to originate with them and to represent them. Sectarian assemblies were now challenged in their class attachment. Furthermore, legality—the authorities legitimised by the Apostle Paul—is now revolutionary. Can sectarian Protestantism still reconcile its desire to cut itself off from the world with its conformism? Will the tension between its social conscience and its religious conscience not reach breaking-point?

This overall situation, if it had become permanent, would probably have led to a very special sort of change. This is a possibility rather than a certainty, and would have affected indigenous sectarian societies more than those dependent on North American assemblies. Even though the experience of Popular Unity lasted only three years, this direction is still interesting to explore.

(i) From dualism towards complementary dichotomy

This possibility would have kept the sect's social system intact, with its totalitarianism and its authoritarian concept of power in particular, but *reinterpreting the basic axis of its ideology*. This would keep its dichotomy, but now as a *duality of complementary terms* rather than a simple dualism; the spirit would no longer be in opposition to matter as the principle of good is in opposition to the principle of evil. They would represent *two distinct levels*, mutually exclusive but both legitimate and complementing one another: the legitimacy of the first would refer to the life of heaven and the needs of the soul; that of the second to life on earth and the needs of the body.

If we look back at the basic paradigm of Pentecostalist ideology (see *supra*, 3 (*b*) (i)) and its possible permutations, all the couplings are preserved with the exception of the last two (Good/Evil, God/Devil). There is no longer a conflict between two powers, but complementarity on two levels. It is no longer an alternative (one *must* choose either the spiritual or the material) but a complementarity: the spirit and the body must co-exist in this earthly life. And even if the first is superior to the second, the second is still legitimate.

Once this point is reached, the Pentecostalist movement could, as a whole, have taken on a political dimension. Its pre-millenarianism could have been kept, but waiting for the other kingdom would no longer have militated against active participation in improving the present one.

Till now, this possibility has been studied as a logical one in theory. But two empirical facts give it historical validity:

1. This type of sect does exist. My study of Protestant groups has brought three examples to light. The most important is the Wesleyan Pentecostal Church, founded by Victor Manuel Mora, who was also very active in the Socialist Party of Chile. Membership of this Church implies being a socialist as well. This Church is rooted in the coalfields of Lota-Coronel (in the Zone of Concepción), and not by accident. In this area, where industry is run down and there is also strong population pressure as a result of migrations from the hinterland, Pentecostalism and Marxism rub shoulders. This, the heartland of the Marxist Left, is the only place where Pentecostalism has taken root among the *working classes*. The particular infrastructure of the region and the part played by a strong personality (Mora) both help to explain why a sect of this sort has appeared here rather than elsewhere.

If I stress the historical existence of this type of sect, it is because the presence of *models* can be an aid to change. And the state of affairs in the country at this time, particularly if it had become established, could have made the example of such a model contagious.

2. The second example is drawn from another country, Cuba, where the growth of sects had only reached an embryonic stage before the success of Castro's revolution. Although my knowledge of this country is limited, I have come across this type of sect there, and the change would seem to be increasing as the years go by and the Castro regime gives evidence of its power to survive and its stability.

(ii) Other possibilities

This direction of change is a real possibility, but so is its antithesis: a *hardening of the dualism* faced with a world becoming that of the 'communist Antichrist'. The religious propaganda emanating from North of the Rio Grande—and from some of Chile's neighbours—certainly worked on these lines, calling for a holy crusade which, under the guise of a care for souls, undoubtedly had other interests at heart. This other possibility is also a real one, and is now coming about. The die is cast!

The final hypothesis about this period is that the 'transition' of Chilean society might not have come about; the regime could have got stuck in 'populist' reformism, drawing back from crossing the true revolutionary Rubicon. In this case, the effect on Pentecostalism would have been rather like that of the earlier period of Christian Democracy.

(c) The military dictatorship: the return of imperialism and dualist hardening

On 11 September 1973, a military uprising put a bloody end to the Government of Popular Unity. The attempt to disengage Chile from the capitalist system and effect a peaceful transition to a socialist society was at an end. The new regime is the creation of the Army. It has the support of the old land-owning oligarchy, determined to get its property back, and of the 'consumerist' bourgeoisie. It also has the—opportunist and circumstantial—support of the urban middle classes and the upper echelons of the working classes.

On the ideological level, the regime claims to be Christian, and even to be restoring Christendom. It expounds ideas very acceptable to the conservative Protestant belt of the United States, well known to be the main financial support for crusades of evangelisation in South America. Pentecostalists, as we have seen, do not go along with an ideal of Christendom: they are waiting for the Kingdom. But they share a dualist view of the world with the military. The 1973 *coup d'état* produced a new situation for them, of which the following are some of the elements:

(i) The years of Christian Democrat government, and even more so those of Popular Unity, had produced an increasing social consciousness and feeling of belonging to a class among Pentecostalists. The generation of charismatic leaders, strongly anti-communist, had still to take account of the new legality operating in society and the hopes and aspirations of the Pentecostalists themselves in that society. The researches of J. Tennekes (1978) clearly show the growing affinity between the *evangélicos* and the Popular Unity Front. But now comes the *coup* and the fall of that Front. The Pentecostal God is an active God, who makes his presence felt in daily life through his spirit, called *el poder de Dios* (God's power). The end of Allende, deciphered according to the code of apocalyptic language, is the expression of this power, the sign of God's will, an expression of his punishment. It is thus a proof of the divine anti-socialism. Woe to those who succumbed to the Marxist temper!

So the event proves that Marxism is the reign of the Evil One *par excellence*, the Prince of this World: 'Marxism, the ultimate expression of the satanic power of darkness', as the Pentecostalist leaders declared in *Mercurio*, 19 December 1974. By the same token, the installation of the military regime gave the old generation of charismatic leaders the chance of re-affirming their hold over the faithful by pointing to the overthrow of those false prophets, sowers of discord, and by restoring the most conservative interpretation of pre-millenarianist dualism.

(ii) But at the same time as the military *coup d'état* put an end to the potential for change of the Pentecostal communities, while restoring their original social structures and ideologies, it created conditions under which religious leaders could acquire greater prestige. The military regime claims to be Christian. But it has serious differences with the Catholic Church, which was very bound up with the political developments of the previous ten years. So the new regime looks to other spiritual forces in the country for approval.

In one of my earliest articles on Pentecostalism (1968), one paragraph was headed, *'imitatio ecclesiae catholicae'*. I wrote then of the decision taken by one of the main Pentecostal movements to build a cathedral 'bigger than the Catholic one', and analysed the way this decision was presented. What was clear was the extent to which the Catholic Church served as a reference point, and the strength of the desire to acquire its status and stop being just a church of the have-nots. Six years later, in September 1974, a year after the *coup*, I stayed briefly in Santiago and was able to see the preparations for the inauguration of the cathedral, which was to take place at the end of the year.

15 December 1974: 'During a ceremony attended by the Supreme Head of State, General A. Pinochet, the temple-cathedral of the Methodist Pentecostal Church of Santiago . . . was solemnly inaugurated. . . . Also present at the ceremony were the Minister of the Interior, General C. Benavides, the Commander of the Santiago Garrison . . . the Chief of Staff of National Defence . . .' (*Mercurio*, 16 December 1974).

19 December 1974: 'Declaration: The Chilean Evangelical Church is today proud that, for the first time in its hundred years of existence, a Head of State has officially received its authorities, pastors and leaders, thereby acknowledging the spiritual force made up of 15 per cent of the Chilean population. . . . Today, we take the opportunity of witnessing to God our gratitude for delivering us from Marxism thanks to the *pronunciamiento* of the armed forces, in which we recognise the wall of protection which God has built against atheist impiety. But we are convinced that Marxism can only ever be completely overthrown by Jesus Christ, since he alone can change men's hearts. This is why we are here, to support our government in its courageous and determined fight against Marxism and to offer it our spiritual collaboration' (*Mercurio*, 19 December 1974).

This proclamation, of which the above is just an extract, covers a whole page of *Mercurio* (including the quote from St Paul about submitting to the lawful authorities) and it is signed by the leaders of the main Pentecostal Churches. Here, at last, is the seal of social approval: 'for the first time . . . a Head of State has officially received its authorities . . .'.

But at the same time the Pentecostal leaders can see the unique opportunity presented to them in the Chile of the military dictatorship. Now that the other great ideology of hope, Marxism, is outlawed and its followers persecuted, now that the economic situation is getting worse and is going to become intolerable for most of the population, Pentecostalism will be left alone to carry its message of salvation, with Caesar's seal of approval. Here is the renewed application of a thesis propounded above: when the popular classes lose their possibilities of social and political participation, then Pentecostalism's chances of growth increase.

CONCLUSION

(*a*) The relationships between Pentecostalism and politics in Latin America are marked by the underlying tension between adherence to a social class (classes) and a system of representations and beliefs.

This system of representation is a 'functional' and effective response to the class situation, when the socio-political system rules out any plan for social change. On the other hand, the tension shows when the system is open to a dynamic of change, be this reformist or revolutionary. When this happens, the pressure of external factors, relayed by this basic characteristic, both internal and external, of the social adherence of the faithful, tends to polarise the community into one 'hard and pure' wing and another capable of producing a reformulation (or rather 'resignification') of the central axis of its representational system.

(b) From the methodological and theoretical point of view, the perspective adopted here postulates the truism—too often neglected—that the evolution of a social group depends at the same time on both factors internal to it (endogenous) and external to it (exogenous).

A social group has a structure. Understanding of this structure, and of its principal links with its environment, allows one to make out the main lines of its dynamic, conceived not as a unique evolutive profile but as a field of possibilities in which one channel often offers the greatest chances of realisation. But changes in the environment (this term is used for convenience, meaning not just 'surroundings', but something that also affects the social group in question) obviously affect the social group. This is why I attach particular importance to the cultural system of the social group. This does not react mechanically to outside events: it interprets them by giving them meaning according to its own code.

This proceeding leads me back to the question of prediction. I would claim that deep knowledge of a *social group* (in this case Pentecostalism) *and* of its *environment* (in this case the social group in which it exists, Chilean society seen as part of a still wider system) allows one to:

(i) put forward propositions about their respective dynamics;
(ii) by formulating hypotheses on changes that can take place in the environment, to put forward propositions concerning their incidence on the dynamic of the social group.

Finally, I would claim that generalisation is not impossible, about the basics of situations in which one finds:

(i) this *type* of social group;
(ii) this type of social group in an analogous environment (being careful to use the adjective accurately): for example—Christian and national 'conversionist sects' in 'dependent capitalist societies'.[6]

Translated by Paul Burns

Bibliography

C. Lalive d'Epinay:
1968 'La "conquista" pentecostal en Chile' in *Mensaje* 170 (Santiago)
1969 *Haven of the Masses* (London)
1972 'Sociedad dependiente, clases populares y milenarismo en Chile' in *Cuadernos de la realidad nacional* 14 (Santiago)
1974 'R. Bastide et la sociologie des confins' in *L'Année sociologique* 25/1975
1975 *Religion, dynamique sociale et dépendance* (Paris/The Hague)
1978 'Conformisme passif, conformisme actif et solidarité de classe' in *Social Compass* XXV/1

J. Medina:
1964 *Consideraciones sociológicas sobre el desarollo económico* (Buenos Aires)

J. Tennekes:
1978 'Le Mouvement pentecôtiste chilien et la politique' in *Social Compass* XXV/1

B. Wilson:
1958 'Apparition et persistance des sectes dans un milieu social en évolution' in *ASR*, No. 5
1959 'An Analysis of Sect Development' in *An. Soc. Rev.* 24/1

Notes

1. Figures derived from population censuses.
2. Is there in Chile a discontinuous line—such as H. Desroche likes to point out—leading

   (*a*) from the Pentecostal strategy based on the face-to-face community to
   (*b*) the Catholic Church's pastoral concept of the 'base communities', and finally to
   (*c*) the *campamentos* strategy pioneered by the MIR but now adopted by all the parties of the left?

There is at least a chronological sequence. . . .

3. This picture is not a Latin American creation, but part of a series of prints distributed by the Bible Societies. So it is understandable that it does not express the whole ideology of sectarian Protestantism, and also contains elements foreign to it, such as a latent bibliolatry—the ray falls on the book rather on the isle as a whole!

4. This is what Pentecostalism calls the Holy Spirit. It is not so much an abstract concept as a reflection of everyday religious experience. Shades of Durkheim!

5. When, to one of my questions, a pastor cried, *'Dios nos permitió salir de este mundo, no es pa'que volvamos adentro'* ('God didn't let us get out of this world just so's we could get back in again') he was not expressing just a dogma, but a fear, one springing from the everyday experience of the world of the dominated in a dependent situation: dole, hunger, sickness, death.

6. This article is of course not predictive. I can boastfully say that I think my earlier works will convince the reader that their timid predictions have been proved accurate enough. Furthermore, it is easy to draw propositions about future developments from this analysis of the past fifteen years.

Clive Dillon-Malone

New Religions in Africa

FOURTEEN YEARS have already passed since it was pointed out that over 5,000 religious bodies had become established in sub-Saharan Africa independently of the mission churches and that at least another 1,000 were on the point of becoming so established.[1] Similar movements have also been noted with reference to Islam.[2] The first reference above was to movements of more specifically Christian orientation and was described as merely the 'tip of the iceberg' whose gigantic mass had not yet broken surface. The overall continental phenomenon has come to be referred to as the African Independent Churches Movement (AICM) and the individual religious bodies as African Independent Churches (AICs). Leaders of these churches have tended to prefer the title of African Indigenous Churches in order to emphasise local initiative and creativity as well as independence from the mission churches. It should be noted that the use of the term 'churches' here does not refer to the sociological usage of the church-sect typology for indeed a great many of these religious bodies exhibit characteristics which are far more typical of the sect. The term is used in so far as these bodies exist as communities which cater for the spiritual needs and the total life-situation of their followers. They furthermore wish to be referred to as churches themselves.

It is not possible to estimate with any degree of accuracy the total numbers involved in such movements which can range from as small a membership as fifty to as large a membership as 500,000. What is clear is that the scale on which the new religions have emerged in Africa within the past 100 years or so is a unique phenomenon in African history. Far from showing any signs of abating, this phenomenon of religious independency has continued to grow and expand over the years involving millions of Africans who for one reason or another have either not felt at home in the mission churches or have not felt drawn to them.[3]

It has been common practice to place the analysis of the AICs within the framework of assaults consciously or unconsciously levelled against African traditional social life and culture by the intruding powers from the western world. The latter included not only colonialists but also missionaries whose Christian religion was so often interpreted as the secret religious force behind the superior power of the white man. This is not surprising in view of the emphasis given to the influence of the spirit world in the African traditional world-view. The growing impact of the more secularised western world-view with its accompanying emphasis on modernisation and technology did much to undermine the relative stability of African traditional socio-religious structures and patterns of life. Colonial power structures, the redistribution of land, the introduction of a cash economy and the rapid increase in migratory labour and rural-urban mobility all contributed to the weakening of traditional authority structures. The extended family system and the position of women in particular was threatened by the missionary condemnation of the socio-economic institution of polygamy. In societies in which religion permeated every aspect of life and in which individual identity and fulfilment were inseparably linked with the clan and the tribe, western distinctions of the following kind tended to find an uneasy resting place, viz., the distinction between the natural empirical world and the supernatural spirit world; emphasis on individual personality growth as distinct from tribal belonging; and the separation of different areas of life into clear-cut compartments. Social change and religious change must be seen as different but inseparable aspects of the one overall process of change in African societies.

The AICs have been engaged in the enterprise of constructing new church communities in response to the emergence of new problems for which neither African traditional religious systems nor the western Christian mission churches were able to offer satisfactory solutions. They are mainly of two types which will be referred to as Secession Churches and Spirit Churches respectively. Whereas the characteristic features of the former bear closer affinity to the western mission churches, those of the latter bear closer affinity to African traditional religions as is indicated in the diagram below:

	AICs		
African	Spirit	Secession	Western
Traditional	Churches	Churches	Mission
Religions			Churches

It should be noted that the purpose of this article is not an attempt to evaluate the extent to which the AICs may be authentic expressions of African Christianity. This could only be achieved through a thorough analysis of individual religious bodies. However, the overall thrust of their socio-religious awareness reveals an undeniably Christian dimension.[4]

The Seccession Churches[5] are the result of mass movements out of the established mission churches. Although the actual schism may take place rather suddenly, it is usually the outcome of a growing discontent with white rule among the membership which reflects the political slogan of 'Africa for the Africans'. These churches, however, do not contain any form of racial enmity, but rather express the demand for self-rule and self-determination. Indeed, some of them have since reunited with the now autonomously-controlled established Christian churches. They tend to remain fairly orthodox in doctrine and worship and to a large extent imitate the forms of organisational structure of the parent churches. However, this tendency to replicate pre-existing church patterns very often conceals the much deeper and more subtle process of transformation which they undergo in practice. There is much greater sensitivity to the cultural expression of religious felt needs and aspirations and western symbols are injected with new meaning. In response to the socio-economic situation of so many of their members, some of these churches either allow or tolerate the practice of polygamy. Doctrinal questions are seldom an issue in the origin of these religious bodies—although in a few cases, they have not been absent. Nevertheless, the almost instinctive emphasis on pneumatology has tended to far outweigh the emphasis on Christology. The reason for this will become more clear as we move into a discussion of the second type of religious body in the AICs, the Spirit Churches. If much greater space and attention is given to the discussion of these churches, it is not because they might seem to be more numerous or more important than the Secession Churches. It is rather because they express more clearly the creative manner in which African traditional socio-religious systems are coming to grips with the new Christian religion within the Judaeo-Christian biblical framework.

Before moving to a more detailed examination of the Spirit Churches, mention needs to be made of a variety of syncretistic movements which have arisen in Africa in this century—religious movements which express a variety of responses to the presence of colonialism and western Christianity in Africa but which have remained predominantly non-Christian in orientation. Of the millennial type, some have been more aggressive in their attempt to hasten the complete transformation of society by the use of military weapons; others, responding more realistically to the superior power of the colonial rulers, have resorted to the more exclusive use of religious rituals and symbols as they await the return of the ancestors or the intervention of some supernatural power. Some religious movements have emphasised the importance of a complete return to the ways of the past; others have attempted to give new meaning and life to traditional rituals and symbols. At times, such movements have taken on Messianic proportions. Particular mention ought also to be made here of the widespread occurrence of witchcraft-eradication movements in East and West Africa. All such movements have failed to make the breakthrough in religious orientation to the use of the biblical frame of reference. It is with this in mind that we move to a consideration of the Spirit Churches which—although often containing elements of the above-mentioned characteristics in their initial stages—make a significant shift of religious direction from the traditional African one.

The Spirit Churches[6] are prophet-founded religious movements which draw their followers indiscriminately from the western mission churches and sects and from African traditional religions. As the name signifies, the dominant emphasis is upon the work of the spirit. The standard pattern for the prophet-founder's conversion experience is something like the following, which is a unique blend of Christian and traditional African elements.[7] The founder—usually a lay person who may be male or female—is a person of religious disposition who has had fairly close contact with one or other of the mission churches or sects and has thereby acquired a deep familiarity with parts of the Bible. He mysteriously contracts an illness—a traditional sign of spirit possession—which is believed to result in his death. While dead, he is taken up into the heavens where he meets the biblical patriachs and/or the prophets. He is then baptised by John the Baptist or by Jesus in a river and commissioned to return to earth as the new messenger from Jehovah, the new John the Baptist for Africa. On his return to life, his new identity is confirmed by carrying a Bible, a white cassock and a staff. It is later confirmed by his ability to perform wonders of healing through the power of the new spirit at work in him.

The rapid success of the prophet's preaching is due to the fact that he is not only capable of crystallising in his message the widespread frustrations and felt needs of his own people but he presents them with a solution which is perceived to be both relevant and meaningful. By making a break with, and indeed rejecting traditional religion, he acknowledges the widespread awareness of its inadequacy to cope with new problems. By presenting himself as the new messenger of God sent directly to African peoples, the intermediary role of the white churches is removed and the Bible is appropriated as God's word for Africa. The one spirit of Jehovah which was once at work in John the Baptist and in Jesus for the white races has now taken possession of an African prophet for the benefit of the black races.

The emphasis on healing in many of the Spirit Churches is very strong and it acts as a powerful attraction for new members. Just as traditional authority roles are taken over by leaders in these churches, so the traditional role of diviner-herbalist (witchdoctor) is taken over by the prophet-founder and others. Traditional healers are condemned far more vehemently by the Spirit Churches than was ever true of the misssion churches.

Healing is now brought exclusively through the power of the new spirit of Jehovah which is perceived to be far superior to the power of traditional evil spirits. Witchcraft and sorcery are universal practices in traditional African societies and all kinds of misfortune and illness are attributed to the activity of witches and sorcerers. Indeed the root cause of all illness is traced to the spirit world. Women in particular are more susceptible to the influence of evil spirits due to their inferior status position and greater insecurity in the traditional socio-economic structure. Failure to bear children, the frequent death of their offspring or tensions arising from being a second or third wife in a polygamous marriage result in physiological and psychological symptoms which are perceived to have their origin in spirit activity. The Spirit Churches offer healing of a pneumo-psycho-somatic kind and it is offered within the framework of a new church community. This last point is crucial. The context of new social relationships is vital if the real cause of so many illnesses is to be removed successfully.

In spite of the importance which members attach to psycho-somatic healing in the Spirit Churches, it is by no means the feature which tends to predominate in regular church services. More often than not, therapeutic sessions take place outside of worship services and with small numbers attending. During Sabbath worship services, the narrower concept of psycho-somatic healing through the spirit gives way to the redemptive concept of healing through the saving power of the holy spirit of God. God is believed to reveal himself through the Bible and through the dreams and visions of the prophets. The people respond in prayer and joyful singing. Worship services are perceived as spirit-filled occurrences and incidents of spirit possession and speaking in tongues are frequent. It is not surprising that the western Pentecostal sects have found such a natural breeding ground in the fertile soil of African traditional religions. Singing, dancing, drumming and hand-clapping are among the most common forms of ritual expression in traditional religious ceremonies. Although these are carried out in the Spirit Churches, they are consciously transformed in such a way as not to be associated with the context of traditional usage. The active participation of all members is a notable feature of worship services and this is carried out in a lively and spontaneous fashion with special reference to singing.

Sabbath worship may last for as long as six hours and the casual and relaxed attitude of members tends to conceal the organisation which underlies the procedure. Preachers, prophets and Bible readers have all been assigned their work beforehand and choirs are free to lead the congregation in singing at whatever points in the ceremony they consider appropriate. The continual interlocking of different activities gives great variety to the overall service. Preaching can vary from brief comments on Bible passages to sermons which can last for an hour or more. There can be as many as four preachers during a service and the most senior preacher normally comes last. Certain prophets—male or female—may speak at any time that the spirit inspires them.

The centrality of the Bible in the Spirit Churches and the manner in which it increasingly becomes the basis and framework of a new character for life indicates a major shift in the traditional African religious outlook. Indeed the more widespread availability of the Bible in the vernacular has been one of the dominant factors in the rise of these churches.[8] In spite of the selective manner in which it is used and the literalistic and fundamentalistic fashion in which it is interpreted, it has introduced an historical and trans-tribal dimension into religious thinking which is of major significance. The socio-cultural background of the Old Testament in particular bears a meaningful resemblance to the traditional African socio-cultural world-view and the pedagogy at work acts as an acceptable and viable means for responding to current processes of social change. Dreams and visions are recognised channels of communication with the spirit world; witchcraft and sorcery are strongly condemned; polygamy is an accepted custom. The one God Jehovah brings salvation and healing to his people through his spirit. Attention, however, is by no means restricted to the books of the Old Testament and the New Testament introduces a religious pattern of thinking which allows for easier adjustment to the process of secularisation.

This article has restricted its scope to a large extent to a consideration of the AICs—the Secession and Spirit Churches—among the new religions of Africa. This does not deny the existence of a whole range of religious movements of a millennial, Messianic or nativistic type which have manifested a wide variety of diverse responses to the wider process of social change which African societies have been undergoing in this century. It does focus, however, on movements which have been demonstrated on a continental scale more manifest signs of consistency in the nature of their response.

It is not easy to pinpoint with any great accuracy the precise cause or causes for the emergence of these churches. Religion and religious movements neither originate nor survive in a social vacuum and political and socio-economic factors are seldom irrelevant to their emergence and their subsequent course of development. In the rise and development of the AICs, racial discrimination and economic exploitation have been stressed by some. Others have emphasised the role of these movements as forerunners or substitutes for political nationalist organisations. On the other hand, the continued growth and expansion of such movements in post-independence Africa has tended to question the sufficiency of explanations of a more political type. Others again have stressed more specifically spiritual elements and the widespread felt need for more culturally satisfying modes of religious expression. What is clear is that the fulfilment of traditional African religious aspirations is not perceived in isolation from the total existential life-situation of the societies to which individuals belong.

The African traditional world-view and African traditional religion(s) have been referred to many times in the course of this article. The intention has never been to suggest any form of static situation in the past for African traditional socio-religious systems have always been undergoing their own dynamic of change prior to the arrival of Christianity in Africa. The data available, however, points to the more powerful degree to which such systems have been disrupted in twentieth-century Africa by the inroads made by colonialism, Christianity and the process of secularisation. The AICs are functioning today as new and more viable socio-religious communities in which millions of individuals can find security, identity and a sense of belonging. This is particularly important for women and for the large numbers who find themselves uprooted from their extended families in search of labour in the urban areas. The AICs cushion their largely uneducated membership from the more direct impact of forces of modernisation by enabling them to cope in a manner and at a pace more suited to their capacity for change. Finally, their missionary enthusiasm renders them important agents of evangelisation in the Christianisation of Africa.

Notes

1. See D. Barrett *Schism and Renewal in Africa* (London 1968). See also the seminal work of B. Sundkler entitled *Bantu Prophets in South Africa* (Rev. ed. London 1961).

2. See H. Fisher 'Independency and Islam: The Nigerian Aladuras and some Muslim comparisons' *Journal of African History* 11 (1970).

3. For a very helpful introduction to the overall phenomenon from different points of view, see H. W. Turner *Religious Innovation in Africa* (Boston, Mass. 1979).

4. Due to the extraordinary variety and complexity of types of religious movements in Africa, attention in this article has been largely focused upon those of more clearly defined Judaeo-Christian orientation. For a comprehensive bibliography of the total range of religious

movements, see R. C. Mitchell and H. W. Turner *A Bibliography of Modern Religious Movements* (Evanston 1966). This list is brought up to date at regular intervals in the *Journal of Religion in Africa*.

5. See, for example, J. B. Webster *The African Churches among the Yoruba* (London 1964).

6. B. Wilson's use of the term 'thaumaturgical' to refer to the response of these religious movements is not really helpful as it is too comprehensive a term and fails to emphasise important distinctions between magic and religion. See B. Wilson *Magic and the Millennium* (London 1973). For particular detailed studies of these movements, see M. L. Martin *Kimbangu: An African Prophet and his Church* (Oxford 1975); C. Dillon-Malone, SJ *The Korsten Basketmakers: A study of the Masowe Apostles, an indigenous African religious movement* (Manchester University Press for the Institute for African Studies, 1978); and for 'aludura' (praying) churches, see H. W. Turner *African Independent Church* (2 Vols.) (Oxford 1967) (for more theological treatment) and J. D. Y. Peel *Aladura: A Religious Movement among the Yoruba* (London 1968) (for a more sociological treatment).

7. For example see Dillon-Malone, the work cited in note 6, pp. 11-18.

8. See Barrett, the work cited in note 1, pp. 127-134.

Arnulf Camps

New Dialogue with Hinduism in India

IN THIS contribution we restrict ourselves to a study of a new approach to Hinduism in India in the form of dialogue as far as it is manifest in the Catholic community. We do so for several reasons. The Catholic community is rather large (10,528,912 members in 1981[1]) and there have been quite a number of significant experiments in the field of dialogue during recent years. Moreover, we are well informed about what is going on in this group of Christians. On the national level the Catholic Church is well organised and in possession of good lines of communication with the rest of the world. The same is not true in the case of the Protestant and Orthodox churches. This does not mean that in those churches no dialogue is being pursued. Our information is, however, casual. A more practical reason for limiting our attention to the Catholic community is that a limited space is permitted to us for this publication.

Some clarification is needed in relation to the question of why new dialogue with Hinduism is being placed under the heading of 'new religious movements'. Usually this topic is not included in this kind of study. A double reason for doing it all the same may be given. The Catholic community in India is not without dynamism. The Catholic Bishops' Conference of India is one of the oldest of the whole Catholic Church as it dates back to the middle of the Second World War[2] and at an early date after the Second Vatican Council in 1969 a kind of pastoral council, attended by more than 600 members of the clergy and the laity, was held.[3] Both helped the church to open herself to Indian culture and to dialogue with the great religions of the country. Thus it was possible for a new religious movement to be born within the Church. A second reason for dealing with this new religious movement in this issue of *Concilium* is to be found in the fact that the effects of this new dialogue with Hinduism are becoming very visible in the life of the Church. People interested in Indian culture and religiosity in other parts of the world could profit by getting acquainted with these new developments.

In this contribution we deal with four aspects of this new religious movement. First, a study will be made of the collective thinking of the Indian church. Secondly, we discuss the national secretariat for dialogue with Indian religions, then, the Indian Eucharist Celebration, which is one of the most salient features of this new life of the Indian Church. In the fourth place, the ashram movement will be studied. Finally, we try to evaluate this new religious movement.

1. THE COLLECTIVE THINKING OF THE INDIAN CHURCH

This collective thinking is expressed through these official documents: (*a*) the Declaration of the Seminar on the Church in India Today, Bangalore 1969; (*b*) the Declaration of the Nagpur Theological Conference, Nagpur 1971; (*c*) the Declaration of the All-India Consultation on Evangelisation, Patna 1973; and (*d*) the Communication of the Catholic Bishops Conference of India to the Roman Synod 1974.[4] It should be mentioned here that this collective thinking came into being after a consultation of the entire church: laity, religious, priests, theologians and bishops.

The Indian church started out with two attitudes towards the great religions in the country: on the one hand, the attitude of the early missionaries who possessed a very negative and superficial attitude toward other religions and on the other hand the attitude of the writers of theological manuals who had no personal knowledge of these religions. Today the Church acknowledges the presence of Christ in other religions and even the saving presence of Christ. The self-communication of God is—according to this Church-teaching—not confined to the Judaeo-Christian tradition, but can be extended to others also. There is one divine economy expressing God's self-communication in different ways and degrees. Finally, it is stated in this collective thinking that an adherent of other religions is saved in his own religion and not in spite of his religion. Thus the founders of the Indian religions and the sacred scriptures of these religions were valued in a positive way.[5] This does not mean, that the Church surrenders the Christian belief in the uniqueness of the Christian economy of salvation. The Church possesses the decisive Word spoken by Christ to the world and the means of salvation instituted by him. Implicitly the difference between absoluteness and uniqueness is admitted. It seems to us to be more important to stress the consequences for a Christian approach towards other religions: the relation between Christianity and other religions should be expressed in positive and inclusive terms, the Church has to learn from other religions, dialogue and contemplation are to be practised, and the ashram movement is a very efficient way to live this new attitude.

This collective thinking of the Indian church is the foundation of a new approach towards the reality of the great Indian religions, especially towards Hinduism. The effects of this new attitude will be studied in the following points of this contribution. However, it should not be supposed that this collective thinking stopped after 1974. We are well aware of the fact that there is a discussion going on among the Catholics of India concerning this positive attitude. We will return to this point at the end of this article. But the line of positive thinking is not dead. A proof may be the Seminar entitled 'The Indian Church in the struggle for a new society', held in 1981[6].

2. THE SECRETARIAT FOR DIALOGUE OF THE INDIAN BISHOPS' CONFERENCE

Dialogue in India is no longer a theoretical matter. Thanks to the continuous endeavour of the leader of the secretariat for dialogue of the Indian Bishops' Conference, Father Albert Nambiaparambil, CMI, dialogue has become a feature of the daily life of the church.[7] Fr. Nambiaparambil is convinced that inter-religious dialogue is the answer of the Christian faith to the saving presence of God in other religious traditions and that is also a sign of our firm hope and expectation that all things will be fulfilled in Christ. Through dialogue integral salvation is to be accomplished for all men. There is no distinction between dialogue and mission. Dialogue is a better name for mission. Through dialogue the Indian church should become Indian and through dialogue non-Christians can find the fulfilment of their deepest aspirations in Christ.

The secretariat for inter-religious dialogue has taken three steps. The first step has been to organise get-togethers. These last two or three days. The participants come from a certain region and most of them are Catholics. A few members of non-Christian religions or ideologies are present. The intention of these meetings is to help the participants to become more able in matters of dialogue. The nature, the object, the conditions, the difficulties, the perils and the possibilities of dialogue are studied. At the end of the meeting very practical steps are proposed. The second step taken by the secretariat for dialogue is the origination of live-togethers. The first took place at Benares in 1973 and the participants were Hindus and Christians. Later also Muslims and Sikhs joined the meetings. The main features of the live-togethers are common prayer, common meditation and common reflection on the meaning of religion in life. All really live together and all pay for the expenses. During several days themes were discussed such as what is the meaning of my religion for me?, what is my relation towards other religions?, what is the role of prayer, religious experience and meditation in my life?, what is the contribution of my religion towards the social needs of my neighbours?, how is my religion challenged by others?, what hope do I cherish?, am I willing to foster mutual unity?, how could we join hands in doing away with Indian caste communalism?, and am I prepared to work together with people of other faiths? It is known that especially these meetings, which lasted for several days, had a deep and transforming influence on believers of all religions. The third step has to do only with the relations between Christians and Muslims. There are in India some 70,000,000 Muslims and the relations between Muslims and Christians have never been particularly good. Fr Nambiaparambil noticed much ignorance between the two groups of faithful. He started courses on Islam and he did so together with the Protestant Henry Martin Institute at Haiderabad. The course takes three days and much information is given. Islamic leaders are invited to attend and the participants take part in a Muslim prayer-service. These courses are held all over India.

It should be noticed here that not only Catholic Christians but also Christians of other denominations take part in the get-togethers, the live-togethers and in the Islamic seminars. The intention to put the responsibility for dialogue in the hands of local Christian communities was fully realised. Out of these experiments ashrams, centres for dialogue and local groups continuing the initiative grew. There are also mixed commissions of several religions fostering cooperation in matters of spirituality and social action.

3. THE INDIAN EUCHARIST CELEBRATION

We may give a brief history of the origin of the Indian new order for the Holy Eucharist before expounding its contents.[8] When in 1963 the Fathers of the Second Vatican Council gave their agreement to the renewal of the liturgy, nobody in India expected such a thing. People were satisfied with the existing Latin, Syro-Malabar or Syro-Malankar rites. However, the bishops started a movement of renewal, as they were well aware of the fact that the improvement of the social condition of the people and a real dialogue with other religions were impossible without the inspiration given by the mystery of Christ. Bishop Lourdesamy became the moderator of the National Liturgical Commission and his brother Father D. S. Amalorpavadass the director of the National Biblical Cathechetical and Liturgical Centre in Bangalore. This centre was and is the great inspiration of many renewals in the church. Seminars and meetings were held. Slowly the *theology of adaptation*, which limits changes in the liturgy to externals, was overcome and the *theology of inculturation* of *contextualisation*, which takes a creative stand in accepting the effects of the dialogue with Hinduism in setting us a meaningful liturgy, was accepted. Two-thirds of the Latin-rite bishops accepted many changes in the liturgy that were still rather external and the proposals were sent to the commission in Rome in charge of executing the Constitution on the Liturgy. The answer was positive and contained even an approval to experiment with a really Indian anaphora. Rome asked that the faithful be prepared by means of very good catechetical instructions. It should not be forgotten that already at this stage there was some opposition among the faithful. Some of them considered the changes to be a turn towards making the liturgy of the Church a kind of Hindu liturgy. Due to the efforts of Father Amalorpavadass most of the believers came to accept the ideas of renewal and to see, that they involved a legitimate inculturation and not a surrender. All the Bishops accepted the adaptation-changes and they supported the creation of an Indian anaphora. At the beginning of the 1970s, a commission started to work on a new order for the Indian liturgy and on an Indian anaphora. However, the opposition grew. In the north of the country the faithful did not oppose changes, as they are a very small minority living in the midst of a Hindu majority, but in the south where most of the Catholics live opposition became powerful. These Catholics have been members of the church for several centuries and they are very much attached to the Latin liturgy. The main points of the opposition were the use of non-biblical scriptures and the Indian anaphora.[9] The opposition was able to influence some bishops, quite a few faithful and, after 1975, also Rome. In that year the use of non-biblical scriptures and of the Indian anaphora was forbidden, though the hard work of the commission was praised. The work, however, in commissions and in congresses went on. Today the new order of the Indian Mass, published in 1974, is used in many experimental services.[10]

The detailed study of the new orders of the Mass for India, published for private circulation and experimentation, is very helpful in understanding the great changes proposed. The reception and welcome of the celebrant is completely Indian. Hands and feet are washed before entering the place of worship. Sandal paste is put on the forehead. The offerings are brought to the altar. The priest greets the community by using the following words: 'Fullness there, fullness here, from fullness fullness proceeds; once fullness has proceeded from fullness, fullness remains.' The purification rite is very Indian: it is a withdrawal of the worshipper as a part of the whole cosmos and a recentring on God. Man and world should convert to God and this is done through concentration. Holy water is used to sprinkle the worshippers. After this the celebrant invites all to renew their life and to exchange the sign of peace. The lamp is lightened as now Christ is present among the people. The second part is the liturgy of the word. Homage is paid to the holy books. First an Indian scripture is read and after that the Indian prayer is said: 'From the unreal lead me to the real, from darkness lead me to light, from death lead me to immortality.' After that the Old Testament, a text from the Apostles and from the Gospel is read. There is ample time for reflection and meditation. The liturgy of the Eucharist is started with the offering of flowers, gifts for the poor, and of bread and wine. The Eucharist prayer has a short and a long version. We follow the long one. The main characteristic of this Indian anaphora is that it maintains continuity with the essential elements of a genuine Judaeo-Christian tradition of liturgy and tries to express at the same time the Christian thanksgiving in forms and thought-patterns harmonious with the Indian culture and drawing from the religious traditions of the country. Frequent acclamations are used. The original language of the anaphora is an Indian one, but there is an English version too. A few quotations may illustrate this English text.

The Indian anaphora is a praise of God's work in creation through creation as a revelation to men, of God's word through patriarchs and prophets and of God's coming among us in the person of Jesus of Nazareth. But the old seers of India are included in this line of communications between God and men:

God of the nations,
You are the desire and hope
of all who search for you with a sincere heart.
You are the Power almighty
adored as Presence hidden in nature.
You reveal yourself
in the seers in their quest for knowledge,
to the devout who seek you through sacrifice and detachment,
to every man approaching you by the path of love.
You enlighten the hearts that long for release
by conquest of desire and universal kindness.
You show mercy to those who submit
to your inscrutable decrees.[11]

After the institution-narrative this intercession is to be found:

We pray you, Father,
crown the yearnings of this our ancient land
with the knowledge and love of your Son.
Bless the efforts of all those who labour
to build our country into a nation
where the poor and the hungry will have their fill,
where all people will live in harmony,
where justice and peace, unity and love will reign.
Bless also our brethren.
who are not present at this Eucharist.[12]

The following doxology may be quoted here:

Amen. You are the Fullness of Reality,
One without a second,
Being, Knowledge, Bliss!
Om, Tat, Sat![13]

We have the impression that we possess here a really Indian anaphora, a real synthesis of Judaeo-Christian and of Hindu traditions. We regret that we are not in a position to give a more complete impression of this rich and—also for western believers—enriching liturgy.

4. THE ASHRAM MOVEMENT

Authors distinguish between three kinds of ashrams: the ancient Hindu ashrams of the classical type which seem to have become extinct in the sixth century AD, the modern Hindu ashrams founded by Mahatma Ghandi, Tagore and Vivekananda, great leaders of modern India on the road to independence and renewal, and the Christian ashram movement.[14] This Christian movement is an attempt to give India an Oriental Christ. Most of the former missionaries did not succeed in doing this. The year 1921 is considered to be the beginning of this Christian ashram movement of the integration of religious life into the Indian context. The names of Dr Jesudasan and Dr Paton are connected with this for ever. Soon the initiative was taken over by many Catholics and Protestants.[15]

In the ashram a Christian lives a kind of contemplative and religious life in continuation of an old Indian tradition. The Indian cultural and religious heritage is assimilated in Christianity in order to make this internally and externally more Indian. The heart of the matter is to attain God-realisation. A missionary doing social work is admired by Indians but not imitated as he lacks the spiritual quest so much appreciated by Hindus. Therefore in the ashrams the Indian ways of attaining this God-realisation, such as yoga, meditation and contemplation, are followed. In opposition to the ancient ashrams, but in agreement with the modern Hindu ashrams, Christian ashrams consider social service to be a continuation of worship and as an expression of love and solidarity with the people around. Ashrams are places of inter-religious fellowship and encounter. In dialogue a common search for God is striven after and quite a few ashrams have both Hindu and Christian members. In this way the Hindu aversion to the institutional side of the Church is overcome. We would like to call these Christian ashrams a new way of being a Church or a new form of Christian togetherness.[16] Another feature of these ashrams is that witness is more a matter of living than of preaching. Contemplation is considered to be the most relevant witness in the deeply religious context of India. The idea behind all this is not that of planting the Church, but that of making the Christian community understandable to non-Christians. That is why the contemplative life should be marked by simplicity, renunciation, detachment and a life close to the people.

It would take too much space to inform the reader about all the Christian ashrams existing today in India. There is no complete survey available, but from our visits to India we can state that they are innumerable. They represent perhaps the most lasting form of dialogue with Hinduism.

5. AN EVALUATION

New religious movements are to be found all over the world.[17] We have limited our attention to the new dialogue with Hinduism in the Catholic Church in India. Though it is not without opposition in India it is becoming a strong movement. It is a new religious movement as it changes the heart and the structures of the Church. Dialogue with Hinduism, the Indian liturgy and the way of living in ashrams are inter-related and often practised by the same people. It is a reform of the Church and a movement quite distinct from the missionary form of being a church in India. For many Christians in India this new way of being a Christian is much more satisfactory and to many non-Christians it is transparent. We hope that this renewed Christian life in India will become known also outside India. Christians all over the world, and especially in the West, long for a deeper and more satisfying Christianity, wherein values like contemplation, God-realisation, detachment and simplicity will be cherished. The need for a dialogue between these Indian Christians and Christians here is becoming more and more urgent.

Notes

1. *Inde: l'Eglise* Agence Internationale Fides 9.1.1981, no. 3143, 8-10.
2. Th. Pothacamury *The Church in Independent India* (Bombay 1961) pp. 122-127.
3. *All India Seminar: Church in India Today* (Bangalore 1969, New Delhi s.a.).
4. A. Karokaran *Evangelization and diakonia* (Bangalore 1978) pp. 167-186.
5. *Research Seminar on Non-Biblical Scriptures* ed. D. S. Amalorpavadass (Bangalore s.a. 1975).
6. *The Indian Church in the Struggle for a New Society, a Research-Seminar* ed. D. S. Amalorpavadass (Bangalore 1981).

7. A. Nambiaparambil, CMI 'Dialogue in India' in *Vidyajyoti* 39 (1975) 111-126 and in *Journal of Dharma* 1 (1976) 267-283; A. Camps, OFM 'Die heutige Stellung der Römisch-katholischen Kirche zu den nichtchristlichen Religionen' in *Jesus Christus und die Religionen* ed. A. Paus (Graz-Wien-Köln-Kevelaer 1980) 256-257. For information concerning the years after 1976, see *Bulletin Secretariatus pro non christianis* (Citta del Vaticano 1977 and following years).

8. A. Camps, OFM *Geen doodlopende weg, lokale kerken in dialoog met hun omgeving* (Baarn 1978) 51-58; J. van Leeuwen 'De lange weg van een liturgievernieuwing, een overzicht van de liturgische ontwikkelingen in India sinds Vaticanum II' *Communio* 2 (1977) 464-476; J. van Lin 'Op zoek naar een eigen eredienst, Rooms-katholieke kerk in India' *Wereld en Zending* 6 (1977) 26-38; J. Masson, S.J. 'Problèmes pastoraux majeurs dans la chrétienté indienne aujourd'hui' *Nouvelle Revue Théologique* 110 (1978) 418-425; D. S. Amalorpavadass 'Indigenization and the liturgy' *International Review of Mission* 65 (1976) 164-181.

9. See note 5.

10. *New Orders of the Mass for India* (approved by the CBCI Commission for Liturgy), a draft for private circulation and experimentation published 'pro manuscripto' (Bangalore 1974).

11. *Ibid*. 45.

12. *Ibid*. 49.

13. *Ibid*. 50.

14. A. Karokaran, the work cited in note 4, pp. 186-199; L. Fr. M. van Bergen *Licht op het leven van religieuzen, sannyasa-dipika* (Nijmegen 1975); A. Elenjimittam *Monasticism, Christian and Hindu-Buddhist* (Bombay 1969).

15. Vandana *Gurus, Ashrams and Christians* (London 1978).

16. A. Camps, OFM 'New ways of realizing a Christian togetherness in non-western countries' *Internationales Jahrbuch für Religionssoziologie* 5 (1969) 182-194.

17. *Dynamic Religious Movements*, ed. J. Hesselgrave, case studies of rapidly growing religious movements around the world (Grand Rapids 1978).

Jan van Bragt

New Dialogue with Buddhism in Japan

INTRODUCTION

RATHER THAN reporting on the state of the dialogue in Japan, these pages will try to locate it and probe for its meaning in a series of marginal notes. The 'New' in my title is, I believe, meant to link this article with the general theme, *New* Religious Movements. Since this may look like a rather cheap trick, allow me to explain, first of all, how I see these relationships.

Would it be too sweeping a statement to say that the new religious movements pullulating in the West but harking back to eastern traditions are merely the scattered symptoms of a deeper trepidation affecting all present-day culture and religion, owing to the fact that, in our 'global village', hitherto closed and self-sufficient universes are for the first time brought together and impinging on one another? From this point of view, the Buddhist-Christian dialogue—which is, indeed, equally new—is evidently one more phenomenon of that same subterranean upheaval. Thus, bringing the two together might lead to a deeper insight into both. A few remarks seem to be called for:

(*a*) We should not forget that the present-day multilateral encounter of cultures was preceded by a period of unilateral encroachment of expansionist western culture on all the others. Thus, for non-western cultures the situation today does not present the same kind of newness as it does for the West, and is rather experienced as the reflux of a tide: from a period of onslaught of western civilisation to its reverse, the victorious reaffirmation of their own cultural values. In direct application to our topic, we must say that new religious movements, instigated by the influence of another culture, are not so new for the rest of the world. Asia and Africa have for a long time already witnessed the birth of new religions, greatly influenced by Christianity and instigated by the need of achieving meaning in a period of change under the impact of a foreign culture. And for the dialogue this sometimes means that the dialogue partner, still resentful of the 'cultural imperialism' of the West, interprets the new desire for dialogue on the Christian side as simply a change in strategy or as a sign of weakness and, clothing himself in his newly acquired sense of superiority, puts up an intransigent front. Still, for all this, it may be said that the present situation shows the same fundamental newness for us all: for the first time the conditions have been created that enable us to experience one another and to meet *as equals*.

(b) The new religious movements bring home to western Christians something experienced long since and much more intensely by the Christian minorities in the East: the fact of the existence of other great religions besides Christianity; in other words, the reality of religious pluralism and of the (at the least geographical) particularity of Christianity. In so far as they really contribute to that awareness in Christianity and, hence, to involving the universal Church in the dialogue with other religions, these movements must be counted a blessing. In this connection, it may be relevant to note that in Japan, once the initial apprehension of a threat to their own identity wore off, the existence of Christian communities in their midst was rather welcomed by many Buddhists, for the possibility of mutual enrichment this affords. In that line, Keiji Nishitani, a Japanese philosopher of strong Buddhist convictions, once confided to me that he would like to see the Christian churches grow stronger in Japan and, therefore, engage in more vigorous evangelisation.

(c) This brings us to the question whether the idea of a 'Christian dialogue with the new religious movements' is a sound one. The answer is of course 'yes', but there appears to be an important condition, which I would provisionally formulate as follows: In the dialogue with them, the new religious movements should not be considered as entities complete in themselves but always together with their eastern cultural background. In other words, the dialogue with these movements, no matter how important in itself, will find its real object only in the more encompassing dialogue with their cultural matrices, the *philosophia perennis* of Hinduism and Buddhism. I am reminded here of the rather indignant reaction of the same Keiji Nishitani to Harvey Cox's book, *Turning East*: 'But he analyses only wild offshoots of eastern religion and has no eye for the real thing.' Indeed, there are reasons why offshoots of a religious tradition in a different cultural milieu cannot by themselves be considered full representatives of their respective traditions. They tend to be either 'too pure': cut flowers not showing any of the mud of life wherein they originated; or hybrids: the products of hasty accommodation to the new ecological environment. This principle, in its universality, applies of course also, *mutatis mutandis*, to the young churches in non-western milieus.

1. JAPAN'S RELIGIOUS SITUATION

In order to understand what the Christian dialogue with Buddhism in Japan represents, we need to place it against the background of Japan's religious situation. We cannot think of painting here a full picture of that situation, but must at least touch on the following points.

(a) Japan's Position in the Buddhist World

After India and Tibet, Japan might be the third most prolific spawner of new religious movements in the West. Of their names, which have become household words in various western milieus, some, like Zen and Pure Land, indicate traditional Buddhist schools, and others, like Sōkagakkai (Nichirenshōshū) and Risshōkōseikai, are the names of Buddhist-inspired 'New Religions'. All this might make us suppose that Japan's Buddhism is especially alive and vigorous, and that Japan occupies an exceptional position in the Buddhist world. This last proposition is, in fact, true if we understand it rightly: Japanese Buddhism, the final fruit of the eastward drive of Buddhism in its Mahāyāna variety, is exceptional not so much for its purity or vigour, but rather on account of the unique circumstances it finds itself in today.

For more than a thousand years, Japan's Buddhism developed in splendid isolation from its cradle, India, and from its sister movements in the Theravāda countries (Sri Lanka, Burma, etc.). It even came to be estranged, in the four centuries preceding the contemporary period, from those countries to which it owes the transmission of Buddhism, namely China and Korea. During this long and secluded history, Japan developed several forms of Buddhism particularly well adapted to the religiosity of the Japanese. However, some of these schools—especially Zen and Pure Land—can be regarded as further developments of tendencies present already in Chinese and even Indian Buddhism. This short characterisation may sufficiently indicate that there can be no question of Japanese Buddhism being universally recognised as a leader by the other Buddhist countries. However, the exceptional secular situation of Japan makes for the unique position of its Buddhism. Thus, Japanese Buddhism is the only Buddhism of a fully developed, modernised and wealthy country. As a result, no other country can boast a comparable intensity or scientific standard of Buddhist studies, and Japanese Buddhism became the main financier of Buddhist projects all over the world (the spreading of Buddhist 'Bibles', building of commemorative shrines in Indian holy places, etc.). What is more, after the communist take-over in China, Vietnam, etc., Japan's Buddhism can be called the only 'free' Mahāyāna Buddhism in the world. (The cases of South Korea and Taiwan being somewhat special.) The fact that, next to India (with Sri Lanka), Japan appears to be the country where the East-West dialogue is pursued most vigorously, may owe much to the same circumstances.

(b) Buddhism's Position in Japan

Japan cannot be called a Buddhist country in the sense wherein Ireland is called a Catholic and Thailand a Buddhist country: namely in the sense that Buddhism would be the decisive element of its national identity. Although it brought 85 per cent of all Japanese within its orbit, Buddhism always had to co-exist with the Japanese native religion, now called Shinto, which it never succeeded in completely subsuming and which, on the contrary, appears to maintain even today a more direct link with the Japanese identity. To this we must add the fact that Buddhism in Japan does not appear as a unity but as a rich mosaic of many totally independent sects.

Moreover, since the middle of the nineteenth century, Japan has witnessed a 'rushhour of the the gods', i.e., the birth of many new religions. Among the many reasons for this remarkable phenomenon, the above-mentioned destabilising influence of western civilisation cannot be disregarded. While all of these new religions tend to be of a syncretistic nature and many find their main inspiration in Buddhism (cf. above), others betray more or less clearly their Shinto origins (Tenrikyō, Ōmotokyō, Konkōkyō, etc.).

These few brushstrokes may make the following practical remarks more understandable:

(i) The Christian effort at dialogue in Japan, although in fact mainly directed at Buddhism, cannot restrict itself to Buddhism but must equally encompass Shinto and the new religions.

(ii) The mutual relationships among these many religions and sects form an intricate network, which sometimes appears as a subtle power struggle, whose complicatedness is further aggravated by the many tie-ups with economic and political powers. Traditionally (i.e., till the end of the Second World War), these relationships were officially regulated by the State. Since the end of the Pacific War, however, a kind of inter-religious dialogue has developed that seems mainly geared to supplying that now defunct regulating function of the State. Needless to say that the character of this multi-religious dialogue is not necessarily very religious. It often strikes one as, in the first place, diplomatic, and certainly avoids what a westerner would consider to be a necessary part of all dialogue, namely, a talking through of one's differences.

(iii) The Church, too, is necessarily involved in this dialogue and, for reasons we cannot now go into, even enjoys a privileged position therein. We cannot flatter ourselves, however, that this would in itself constitute a real dialogue as envisaged by Vatican II and required by our times. On the other hand, this encounter of the religions requires such an intimate knowledge of the ever-changing situation that a 'Quicksand, danger!' sign should be put up for the benefit of all outsiders (including Roman instances).

(c) Christianity's Position in Japan

Only three relevant traits of the Catholic Church in Japan can and must be mentioned here. To begin with, it is a tiny minority (barely 0·4 per cent, four per thousand, of the population) surrounded on all sides by Japan's diffuse religiosity and powerful religious organisations. Psychologically, therefore, it stands in need of a strong feeling of identity over against these religions; and naturally looks for that identity in 'authentic' and readily recognisable forms. Secondly, a stronghold of the Catholic Church is the district of Nagasaki where the feeling is alive of being the heirs of the Kirishitan martyrs—those martyrs who were persecuted with the strong complicity of some Buddhist sects. And thirdly, most of the Church leaders have never felt the need for theological and pastoral updating thrust upon them by altered circumstances or movements at the grassroots. Indeed, many of the reforms promoted by Vatican II do not make any difference in our missionary situation. Unfortunately, one baby eminently relevant to the Japanese situation—the new and positive evaluation of the other religions—thereby tends to get thrown out with the bath water.

From there, two facts become understandable. Firstly, the dialogue with other religions in Japan, rather than a movement of the Church as such (either in the sense of the Christian in general or of the leaders) towards a new openness to these religions, is mostly, at this stage, the affair of a small but active minority. And secondly, the dialogue has not had any noticeable effect (yet) on the general run of catechesis, liturgy, para-liturgy and other Christian forms. It looks as if, on this point, we are sorely behind what is happening in India.

2. SOME DATA ON THE DIALOGUE WITH BUDDHISM IN JAPAN

We must restrict ourselves here to a bird's-eye view and refer the reader to the bibliography for further detail. Putting aside the more 'diplomatic' dialogue mentioned above, which makes possible a certain degree of collaboration for indisputable causes (world peace, e.g.) and which engendered two organisations with international scope, the *World Conference of Religion and Peace* (WCRP) and the *United World Federalists of Japan*, I want to focus here on the encounters of a more intrinsically religious nature.

On the Christian side, this dialogue is mostly carried on by a few free-lance religionists and scholars and by four institutes: the Protestant *NCC Center for the Study of Japanese Religions* in Kyoto (given its present form in 1959 by Tetsutarō Ariga; director: Masatoshi Doi), and three Catholic centres: *Oriens Institute for Religious Research* in Tokyo (founded in 1959 by Joseph Spae; director: Raymond Renson), *Institute for the Study of Oriental Religions* at Sophia University, Tokyo (founded in 1970 by Heinrich Dumoulin; director: Thomas Immoos), *Nanzan Institute for Religion and Culture* (founded in 1975; director: Jan van Bragt).

F

(a) Encounter on the doctrinal level (philosophico-theological approach)

To be mentioned here, among others, are the *Round Table Conference on Religion* in Kyoto, initiated by the NCC Center and gathering Christians and Buddhists of different schools four or five times a year for a discussion of common problems; the *Conferences on Japanese Religions*, a week of conferences with panel discussion, organised every year by the Sophia Institute around the theme: 'Christianity and . . . (a Buddhist sect or other religion)'; and the *Nanzan Symposia*, which bring together for three days, once every two years, five Christian and five Buddhist scholars for an in-depth discussion of a basic religious topic. There is also the biannual *Conference on Religion in Modern Society* (Cormos), where scholars and leaders of different religions meet to discuss contemporary problems from a multi-religious point of view.

These conferences, however, are only the tip of the iceberg. The above institutes also carry on, in a more quiet way, ongoing dialogues with some Buddhist groups, engage in joint study of Buddhist Scriptures, etc. And anyway, the conferences tend to send the participants back to their studies for a deeper research on the other religion and, maybe more so, an intense theological reflection on their own traditions. Here it must be noted that, in Japan, this more personal research and reflection predates by far our era of inter-religious conferences. Indeed, since the thorough adoption of western civilisation in the nineteenth century, Japan has become a country that falls heir to two completely different cultures, with the result that for its more reflective citizens some kind of synthesis of East and West has become a necessity of life. This has given rise to a substantial amount of literature wherein the Buddhist-Christian relationship is investigated. Outstanding in this field, both for their depth and genuine openness to Christianity are the works of the so-called Kyoto School of Philosophy, of which the main representatives are: Kitarō Nishida (1870-1945), Hajime Tanabe (1885-1962), Keiji Nishitani, Yoshinori Takeuchi, Shizuteru Ueda, and others.[1] Their influence has begun spreading abroad, especially in Germany and the United States.

(b) Encounter on the level of praxis (experiential approach)

Again in the line of conferences, but aiming this time at a sharing of spirituality, there is the *Oiso Conference*, which for fifteen years has been gathering Buddhists (mostly Zen) and Christians every year for sharing of religious experience.[2] There has also been the rather unique *East-West Spiritual Exchange Program* that in September 1979 gave thirty-four Buddhist monks and nuns a chance to share the monastic life for three weeks in Benedictine and Trappist monasteries in Europe.[3] But best-known might be the movement, often called 'Christian Zen', whose initiator was Father Enomiya-Lassalle. It incorporates the Zen form of 'meditation', and often also the *kōan* exercise, into Christian spirituality and organises retreats in Japan and abroad along the lines of a Zen *sesshin*. At a guess (for no statistics are available), it counts a few hundreds of adepts in Japan, mostly Catholic nuns and lay people. It gave rise to two centres of Christian-Zen spirituality, the Shinmeikutsu (of Fathers Lassalle and Kakichi Kadowaki) near Tokyo, and the Takamori Community of Fr Shigeto Oshida in Nagano prefecture. While not recognised as fully Zen by most Zen people, it greatly contributes to the evaluation and adaptation of the contemplative element of Christianity in the Japanese setting.

BY WAY OF CONCLUSION

This all too short treatment of the Buddhist-Christian dialogue in Japan leaves us with many questions: What is the aim of this dialogue and what does it presuppose and imply? How far is the need for dialogue felt by the Buddhists also? How can it become an affair *of* the Japanese Church? And many more. To the question, What is 'new' in the dialogue, I would venture the following answer. The Church is invited now to shed its western provincialism and to actualise its universality in the eastern context. To missionaries and Christians in Japan is given the theological possibility of living their evangelising efforts as an 'exchange in love', with the consciousness of receiving more than one gives. Our Christian converts are given a chance to incorporate their own spiritual past into the newness of Christ's message. And the new willingness of the Church to meet the other religions on an equal basis has already brought about a real change in the perception of Christianity by the others: from arrogant adversary to strong ally-competitor—with for the others the concomitant possibility of receiving from Christianity without loss of face.

However, the 'Encounter with Buddhism' is a Herculean task which cannot be brought to a good end by the 'outposts of Christianity in the East' alone. It is an urgent task for the universal Church and especially for all its theologians. Herein the role of our local institutes can only be that of catalysers and bridges for a two-way traffic.

May this sound as an urgent appeal!

Notes

1. A good insight into the ways of thinking of this school and their relationships to Christianity can be gained from H. Waldenfels *Absolutes Nichts. Zur Grundlegung des Dialogs zwishen Buddhismus und Christentum* (Freiburg/Basel/Wien 1976—English translation by J. W. Heisig *Absolute Nothingness* (New York 1980)).

2. A partial report can be found in *A Zen-Christian Pilgrimage. The Fruits of Ten Annual Colloquia in Japan, 1967-1976* (The Zen-Christian Colloquium, Tokyo 1981).

3. Report to be found in *Japan Missionary Bulletin* 34 (1980) 158-177 and *The Eastern Buddhist* 13 (1980) 141-150.

Bibliography

Works by Joseph J. Spae, the latest of which is: *Buddhist-Christian Empathy* (Tokyo 1980).
Heinrich Dumoulin *Christianity meets Buddhism* (LeSalle, Illinois 1974).
Heinrich Dumoulin *Begegnung mit dem Buddhismus* (Freiburg/Basel/Wien 1978).
Japanese Religions 10 No. 4 (1979) with articles by Yukio Irie, Jan Swyngedouw, Notto R. Thelle, Jan van Bragt.

Richard Bergeron

Towards a Theological Interpretation of the New Religions

IN THE COURSE of the last two decades western society has seen the emergence of a rash of religious phenomena in which we observe the symptoms of a new model of religiosity developing on the fringes of traditional Christianity. These phenomena take extremely varied forms from rigorous asceticism to full-blown hedonism, the cult of Satan, all kinds of witchcraft, spiritism, occultism, parapsychology and westernised orientalism. Scientism, religion and magic unite in an unprecedented way. Brainwashing, exploitation and the will to power exist side by side with genuine conversion and authentic spiritual experience. In this dense, little-explored jungle, it is difficult to discriminate between the true and the false, what is new and what is merely a resurgence of the old, what is a manifestation of a new type of religiosity and what is a syndrome of regression of the religious consciousness to its atavistic and most dubious levels. Are we faced with a divine awakening, a failure of religion or a substitute for the faith?

These are all questions confronting the theologian in the phenomenon of the new religions. Theological discourse on this phenomenon requires a sound knowledge of the territory, an appropriate method of analysis and an insight into what is fundamentally at stake.

1. THE NEW RELIGIONS

After long study of the territory we may say that the new religions can be grouped into two large spiritual families, each with their own particular doctrines and practices and their own sort of mysterious spirituality. The two families have developed side by side and the antagonism they show towards one another suggests deep divergences between them.

The religious groups in the first family base their ideas and their ethical system on the ancient Judaeo-Christian tradition. They regard the Bible as their ultimate source of reference but they interpret it in the light of a subsequent 'revelation' or by particular principles, the most common of which are fundamentalism and concordism. These groups have an eschatologist or millenarist tendency and claim to be directly linked to the early Church by a leap which passes over the rest of history between. They think of themselves as the Church of the pure, they speak the language of decision and

74

conversion and protest strongly against the permissiveness of society and the compromises of the established Church. They have a dichotomistic view of the world and profess a radical discontinuity between the order of creation and the order of grace and an absolute disconnection between the empirical world and the kingdom of God.

Eschatologist or millenarist, evangelical or neo-evangelical, Pentecostalists or neo-Pentecostalist, Bible followers or syncretists, all these groups within the Judaeo-Christian tradition can be defined as 'sects' in Troeltch's sense.[1] These very numerous groups are not what we are concerned with here.

This article is interested only in groups in the second spiritual family. These groups don't find their fundamental symbols and their central ideas in the Judaeo-Christian tradition but turn to the eastern esoteric tradition, Oriental mysticism in ancient religions (druidic, Egyptian, Atlantean, American Indian), parapsychology, humanist psychology and science (or science fiction). They usually appear to be syncretist amalgamations or aggregates of elements borrowed from the most diverse religious, philosophical and spiritual traditions. They have all kinds of names: order, church, society, centre, academy, movement, institute, association, fraternity, union, circle, foundation, temple, group.

Whatever the difference and variety of names, these groups share a fundamental commonalty of attitude, world-view and religiosity. These groups are monist: they propose a vision of the world which considers the multiplicity of beings to be an illusory manifestation of absolute metaphysical unity. All is one. The world is identical with its divine source. There is no distinction between the world and its cause. The world proceeds by emanation. The latter is seen as an involution, a descent, a fall of the divine spirit into matter: the mystery of the incarnation. Man's spiritual journey consists in doing the opposite and it is called evolution, return, elevation of the spirit: the mystery of the ascension. Meanwhile the spirit remains imprisoned in the world of illusion (*maya*) and crucified upon matter: the mystery of the cross. The divine spirit is chained to a degenerescent temporality: cyclic time, closed circle, eternal return, perpetual restarting. Hence the commonly accepted doctrine of *karma* and reincarnation.

Man cannot escape from karmic destiny and the wheel of Samsara except by latching on to higher spiritual energy. This energy is the ultimate tissue of all reality. It is called 'universal', 'spiritual', 'divine', 'Christic', 'conscious', 'mental' or 'cosmic'. The substantial unity of the universe destroys the polarities and resolves the antitheses. The heart of spiritual advance lies in the being drenched with divine energy and its aim is to lead the individual towards harmony with himself and the whole of the cosmos and the attainment of absolute mastery over self, which is the principle of inner freedom.

Primacy is given to the inner life, to spiritual awakening, the exploration of the psyche and the consciousness. The disciple is invited to meditate, to enter into his inner sanctuary, to have psycho-spiritual experiences so that he may know himself. Knowing oneself is knowing God and the cosmos. In this religious universe the language is not of ethics but of mysticism, not of faith but of knowledge, not of eschatology but of protology, not of decision but of experience, not of commitment but of illumination, not of evil but of ignorance. An esoteric and symbolic language is employed, particular importance is given to the feminine principle and to the development of psychic powers as of the Shaman or the healer. Usually there is the postulation of the existence of innumerable super-terrestial spiritual beings who inhabit the space that separates man from divinity.

Everything becomes a matter of consciousness. Contemporary society keeps man on a very low level of consciousness. The liberation of latent energies and sleeping potentialities is through the awakening of consciousness. The expansion of consciousness makes direct contact possible with divine energy. The proposed goal is to reach divine consciousness. This consciousness is called 'cosmic', 'supra-normal', 'Christic', 'superior', 'Buddhic', or 'transcendental'. The experience of these states of consciousness constitutes an essential characteristic, perhaps *the* specific mark of the new religiosity.

One arrives at the experience of cosmic consciousness through the practice of certain techniques inspired by eastern religious or by western therapies, or primitive rites or esoteric sciences. Techniques of meditation and breathing, yoga, certain bodily postures, fasting, mantras, mandalas, special diets, songs, dances, martial arts, etc. These are all disciplines used to lead the disciple to higher consciousness and to blessed states known as 'illumination', 'ecstasy', 'instasy', 'peak experience', 'satori', 'nirvana', 'light'.

In this experience of beatific consciousness, true knowledge blossoms. Knowledge alone, not faith, has saving power. This knowledge is not scientific, philosophical or theological knowledge. It is not the result of reasoning or calculation. It is an experience of communion in which the knowing subject is identified with the object known. In this communion the world is transfigured into the self and fusion takes place with the divine. This knowledge, which is the way to salvation, is given all kinds of different names: 'Christian science', 'spiritual science', 'divine science', 'religious science', 'cosmic science', 'science of the creative intelligence', 'science of the mind', 'spiritual psycho-synthesis', 'theosophy', 'anthroposophy', 'astrosophy', 'artheology', 'primordial knowledge', 'tradition', 'pansophy'.

Among the groups which form the second spiritual family, we may mention by way of example: the Universal White Fraternity, the Theosophical Society, the Anthroposophical Society, the Rosicrucian Association, the AMORC Rosicrucian Order, the Institute of Applied Metaphysics, Eckanar, the International Gnostic Association, the Divine Light Mission, the International Association for the Consciousness of Krishna, Dharmadatu, the Sri Chimnoy Centre, Subud, the Lovers of Meher Baba, the Science of the Mental, the Church of Scientology, the Universal and Triumphant Church, Mahikari, Aumism, the 3 HO Foundation, etc., etc. . . . .

All these groups claim to exist in the twilight of an evil age and at the dawn of a new age. The age of darkness, Kali Yuga, the Age of the Fish, the Church of Peter, the Church of Christ is over. The golden age, the Parousia, the Age of Aquarius, the age of the Apocalypse, the Spiritual Church of John, the invisible Church of the Spirit, the millenium is about to arrive. All the new spiritual groups claim to be mediators of the new age. Their disciples are *mutants* who have reached a state of higher consciousness and are thus capable of being the agents of evolution. They are the small remnant of the perfect who work the great alchemical work of psychic mutation.

In their broad outlines and their type of religiosity the new religions have surprising similarities to ancient gnosticism. We formulate the following hypothesis: *the phenomenon of the new religions constitutes an emergence of the eternal gnosis into our contemporary world, given that gnosis is not a Christian heresy but a particular and original phenomenon of the history of religions.*[2] As a religious type gnosis is a way of inner experience in which man grasps his ultimate truth, remembers his origins and becomes aware of his divine nature. The specific mark of gnosis is the knowledge of the transcendental and divine self imprisoned in the world of appearances. Its secondary characteristics (dualism, esoterism, a-temporalism, antinomianism, the doctrine of reincarnation and higher beings, etc.) group themselves round this central specific characteristic. They follow from it.

2. THE METHOD OF DYNAMIC TYPOLOGY

If gnosis is a specific religious type, if it appears as a particular phenomenon of the history of religions, it should receive particular theological treatment which respects its true nature and its original status within the religious phenomenon in general. The encounter of Christian thought with gnosis is a specific case in the confrontation of Christian with other religions. The new gnostic groups themselves claim a particular status in the history of religions side by side with the established religions. They often refuse to accept the name 'religion'; they consider themselves to be the heart of religion, or rather the universal, primordial, non-temporal religion, of which the established religions are more or less debased exoteric manifestations.

Under the appearance of openness and tolerance the new gnostic groups are making a universalist claim. They feel they possess a truth which is valid for all. Although they are reserved for the perfect, that is to say those who have the necessary qualifications in the present reincarnation, they hold themselves to be the universal way of liberation. Now any group—or person—convinced that it possesses a truth of universal validity implicitly rejects any claim to the contrary. In the order of thought every statement entails *ipso facto* the negation of the contrary claim.

Total rejection goes with the 'biblicist' method practised by evangelical Christianity (*Biblia locuta est: causa finita est*) and the 'dogmatist' method often found in the Catholic Church (*Roma locuta est: causa finita est*). Partial rejection and partial acceptance goes with the so-called 'humanist' method. The criterion of acceptance and rejection is no longer the Bible or dogma but rationality.

We think that rejection should be considered as the dialectical union between rejection and acceptance. Total rejection and total acceptance in the same dialectical movement. What do we mean by this assertion?

We know on the one hand that the gnostic systems, both ancient and modern, are a particular assembly of all the elements that commonly belong to the religious sphere in general and that, on the other hand, the elements constitute polarities within the gnostic system. The elements in isolation are not gnostic because they belong to the universal religious heritage. It is the system within which they are combined which is gnostic. The presence of religious elements held in common with Christianity (ethics, mysticism, salvation, relations with the divine, revelation, etc.) justifies total acceptance. And the system which transfigures these elements by submitting them to the crucible of the gnostic intention requires total rejection.

This is how we justify the principle of the dialectical union of rejection and acceptance which requires a method of analysis by dynamic typology. This method, based on polarities rather than on antitheses, appears to us to be helpful for a Christian understanding of contemporary gnostic groups.[3]

The typological approach goes beyond the level of doctrines to that of principles and the religious experience that these principles require and encourage. Doctrines are changeable but the principles remain. It is the principles which define the configuration of a religious type. The type is a theoretical model, abstracted from any real existing example and it is used to understand another reality presumed to be analogous. The type does not exist anywhere in space or time. What exists is a mixture of types in any single particular example. Every gnostic group is an original incarnation of the gnostic type. The types exist side by side and do not seem to interpenetrate at all. The types appear static as the dynamic element is left to the individual and particular.

But the types are not necessarily static. In each type there are tensions which carry it beyond its own limits. 'Dialectical thought,' writes Paul Tillich, 'has shown the immense fertility of the dialectical description of tensions in structures that appear static. The kind of dialectic most adequate for typological analyses is the description of contrasting poles within a structure. A relation between the poles is a relation of interdependent elements, each being necessary to the other and to the whole by being in tension with the opposite element. Tension leads to conflicts and beyond conflict to the possible union of poles. Described in this way the types lose their static rigidity. Individual persons and things can transcend the type to which they belong without losing their particular character.'[4]

Fundamentally religious types are distinguished from one another less by the elements that compose them than by the articulation of these elements and the tension of these elements within a single model. This is why religious types attract and repel each other both at once. This is very true of gnosis and Christianity. The decisive point in the interpretation of religions is less their (doctrinal, cultural and institutional) historical and contingent structure, than the totality of elements which make up their respective type.

The method of dynamic typology consists in working out religious types, comparing them, showing their likenesses and contrasts and the dialectic of polarities. This method requires a continual coming and going from the particular to the abstract and the abstract to the particular, from the multiple to the one and from the one to the multiple.

The method of dynamic typology becomes a method of theological interpretation when the Christian type is used as the privileged point of reference. Of course no historical (doctrinal or institutional) modality of Christianity can serve as the final arbiter in interpretation because historical modalities are always relative and *semper reformandae*. Only the original type of Christianity beyond its incarnate modalities can be invoked as a key with which to interpret the new religions. We can only grasp the essential type of Christianity through its past and present realisations and its projections into the future. The type does not fall from heaven, it is abstracted from the past, present and future.

3. THE RISKS FOR CHRISTIANITY

The application of the typological method enables us to abstract the polar elements from the gnostic type and to see how the dialectic of these elements functions in actual gnostic groups. It also allows us to do the same for Christianity. The dialogue between gnosticism and Christianity is always accompanied for the Christian by a silent conversation with his own religion. If, for example, the theologian argues with the gnostic about the dialectical articulation of mystical and ethical elements, at the same time he is arguing about it with himself in his own experience and within Christianity.

This is also the case with the dialectic between revelation as experience and as *ex auditu*, between temporality as circularity and as finality, faith as confidence and as knowledge, evil as sin and as ignorance, experience of God as a dialogue of communion and as experience of the self, ethics as sharing in the building of the world or as communion with nature, salvation as a gift of God and as human action. These polarities only actually exist in dialectical tension both in the gnostic groups and in the Christian churches. At this level gnosis and Christianity contain the same religious elements.

The typological method is not confined to the dialectical of polarities; it goes on to the level of fundamental principles which articulate the gnostic type, define its specificity and dictate its doctrinal system. This is where we find the gaps. The convergence of polarities goes side by side with the divergence of principles and experiences. This is where the profound incompatibilities emerge. The gnostic systems which might have attracted the Christian now appear as deeply hostile. At this point Christianity cannot incorporate gnostic principles without changing its nature and losing its specificity. Through the principles which govern them the new gnoses attack the most important principles of Christianity.

It would be easy to show that contemporary gnoses discredit the sacramental, historical and dogmatic principles, which constitute the fundamental axes of the Christian type and define its spirituality and hermeneutics. Current gnostic groups totally reject historical sacramentality in favour of a residue of cosmic sacramentality. In its very essence gnosis tends to transcend all sacramentality. This is because it holds that time and matter are illusory. How can an appearance be a sacrament? The sacramental principle requires the reality of history and the material world. Because time is illusory and consequently evil, gnoses invent their sacraments by myths: legendary or primordial events, astrological coincidences, antediluvian or Atlantean personages. Because matter is illusory and consequently evil, contemporary gnoses invent their 'sacraments' with 'anti-matter': an inarticulate sound (*mantra*), an abstract pattern (*mandala*), an abnormal posture, privation of food or interrupted breathing. Through its conception of time and matter, present-day gnosis shows itself to be fundamentally hostile to the sacramental principle so dear to Christianity.

Furthermore all the gnostic groups agree in rejecting the historical principle which is also so fundamental to Christianity. By its non-temporal conception of revelation and the esoteric principle at the heart of its hermeneutics, gnosis de-historicises everything it touches and transforms historical events into non-temporal myths. History must be transcended. The primordial tradition to which all the gnostic groups refer is preserved on the astral plane which is supra-physical and meta-historical. Gnosis is eternal: it transcends the history in which it sporadically manifests itself through the ages. Contemporary gnoses represent a huge effort to make salvation cosmic: they release religion from its historical anchorage.[5] In this, too, they are taking up a position hostile to an essential dimension of Christianity.

Finally the gnostic groups are fiercely anti-dogmatic. Gnostic revelation is the personal discovery of the truth hidden in the heart of the self. The authentic master—the only one who has the words of life—is the inner *guru*. No objective revelation can be a yardstick by which to judge authentic revelation, which is eternal. The ultimate goal of all objective revelation is to become superfluous and disappear. Experience itself is the final criterion of knowledge and truth. The only truth is what is experienced as true. In the end objective authority and external criteria are disqualified. Thus the dogmatic principle is radically eliminated (this is the principle in Christianity which preserves ecclesial experience in the limits of revelation).

Of course the rejection of the sacramental, historical and dogmatic principles can reach different degrees in different gnostic groups. Essentially all gnosis aspires to transcend them totally, because its ultimate goal is awareness with the self transcendent and in immediate communion with the divine. Everything that mediates experience (history, sacrament, doctrine) is a crutch destined to be cast aside.

All this shows plainly the gulf between Christianity and present day gnostic groups. The metaphysical and cosmic perspective of gnosis completely undermines the historical, sacramental and dogmatic bases of Christianity. A higher synthesis between Christianity and gnosis is only possible if Christianity is submitted to a reduction which would destroy its very nature. A. Watts writes: 'A theology which has to do with dogmatic, historical and sacramental ideas constitutes a totally different view of reality from a metaphysical mysticism and we cannot confuse these two languages without ending up in an inextricable muddle.'[5] Truth requires that we should distinguish in order to unite, both beings and religions.

Translated by Dinah Livingstone

Notes

1. E. Troeltch *The Social Teaching of the Christian Church* 2 vols. (New York 1931).
2. This hypothesis is shared today by a growing number of writers. I have tried to demonstrate it in my book, *Le Cortège des fous de Dieu*. Many new religious groups call themselves 'gnoses' or

recognise their links with the gnosticism of antiquity. Of course certain groups do not fall under this religio-theological type. Note that certain American writers, following Troeltch's typology, speak of 'mysticism', or following Yinger's typology, prefer to speak of a 'cult' to designate what we think is more aptly designated by the term gnosis (J. Milton Yinger *Religion, Society and the Individual* (New York 1957).

3. See Paul Tillich *Christianity and the Encounter of World Religions* (New York 1964).

4. *Ibid.* p. 64.

5. Quoted by B. Chethimattan 'The Scope and Conditions of a Hindu-Christian Dialogue' in *Concilium* 3, No. 1 (March 1965) 83-93.

Contributors

DICK ANTHONY is a psychologist who is a research associate at the Center for the Study of New Religious Movements at the Graduate Theological Union, Berkeley, California. In addition he is in private practice in transpersonal body-oriented psychotherapy. He has published extensively on the mental health effects of new religious movements and has been principal investigator of several funded research projects on that topic. His books include: *In God We Trust: New Patterns of Religious Pluralism in America* (Transaction 1981) which he co-edited with Thomas Robbins; 'Conversion, Coercion, and Commitment' in *New Religious Movements* (Crossroads, forthcoming) which he co-edited with Thomas Robbins and Jacob Needleman; and *Between Religion and the Human Sciences* (University of California Press, in preparation) which he is co-authoring with Thomas Robbins and Robert Bellah.

RICHARD BERGERON, OFM, comes from Charlevoix (Quebec). He has a licence in theology from the University of St Paul (Ottawa) and a doctorate in religious sciences from the University of Strasbourg (France). He has been lecturer in the faculty of theology at Montreal University since 1967. He has published several books on theology, the religious life and the new religions, including: *Les Abus de l'Eglise d'apres Newman* (Montreal 1971); *L'Obéissance de Jésus et la verite de l'homme* (Montreal 1976); *Le Cortège des fous de Dieu* (Montreal 1982).

JAN VAN BRAGT, CICM, was born in Belgium (Flemish part) in 1928, and joined the Scheut fathers (CICM) in 1946. After ordination to the priesthood (1952), he did further studies of philosophy at Louvain Hoger Instituut voor Wijsbegeerte and gained a professorate in the seminaries at Scheut. He gained his PhD in philosophy in 1961, and left for Japan the same year. Between 1965-1967 he was research fellow at Kyoto University, specialising in a study of Buddhism and Japanese thought. Since 1976 he has been director of the Nanzan Institute for Religion and Culture at the Nanzan University in Nagoya. The main articles in connection with the dialogue are the following: 'Notulae on Emptiness and Dialogue' in *Japanese Religions* 4 (1966) 50-78; 'Nishitani on Japanese Religiosity' in *Japanese Religiosity* ed. J. Spae (Tokyo 1970) 271-284; 'Interfaith Dialogue in Japan' in *Japan Missionary Bulletin* 30 (1976) 583-594; 'Tangenten an einem Vollkommenen Kreis?' *Munen Musô. Ungegenständliche Meditation* ed. Günter Stachel (Mainz 1978) 378-396; 'The Interfaith Dialogue and Philosophy' in *Japanese Religions* 10 (1979) 27-45; 'East-West Spiritual Exchange: A Report on a Project' *Japan Missionary Bulletin* 34 (1980) 158-177.

ARNULF CAMPS, OFM, was born in 1925 at Eindhoven, Holland, entered the Order of the Franciscans in 1943, and was ordained in 1950. He gained a doctorate in theology at Fribourg, Switzerland, in 1957. He was professor at the regional seminary of West Pakistan, Karachi, between 1957-1961, mission-secretary of the Dutch Franciscans 1961-1963, in Weert, Holland, and has been professor of missiology at the Catholic University of Nijmegen, Holland, since 1963. He was president of the International Association of Mission Studies between 1976-1980, consultor of the Secretariat for Non-Christians, Vatican, between 1965-1979. He has been president of the Interuniversity Institute for Missiology and Ecumenics in Holland since 1981, and a member of the board of the World Conference on Religion and Peace, New York, since 1979. He does regular study-tours to countries of the Third World. His publications include:

Jerome Xavier SJ and the Muslims of the Mogul Empire, controversial works and missionary activities (1957); *In Christus verbonden met de godsdiensten der wereld* (^{2}1964); *Christendom en godsdiensten der wereld* (1976); *De Weg, de Paden en de Wegen* (1977); *Geen doodlopende weg* (1978); *Christenen in continentaal China vandaag: inzicht en uitzicht* (1981).

JOHN A. COLEMAN, SJ, a member of the board of editors of *Concilium*, was born March 27 1937 in San Francisco. He holds a doctorate in sociology from the University of California, Berkeley and has done advanced graduate studies in theology. He is currently associate professor of religion and society at the Graduate Theological Union, Berkeley, California. Among his books are: *Sociology: An Introduction* (New York 1968); *The Evolution of Dutch Catholicism* (Berkeley 1978); *An American Strategic Theology* (New York 1982).

CLIVE DILLON-MALONE, SJ, was born in Dublin, Eire, in 1938, and did his philosophical and theological studies at the Gregorian University, Rome, and in Dublin, Eire. He received his MSocSc degree from Birmingham University, England, at the Centre for West African Studies and his PhD in sociology from Fordham University, New York. He first came to Zambia, Africa, in 1963. At present, he is Superior of St Ignatius Jesuit Community Parish in Lusaka and lectures in sociology at the University of Zambia. He has had a book published entitled *The Korsten Basketmakers: A Study of the Masowe Apostles, an Indigenous African Religious Movement* (Lusaka 1978).

ROBERT S. ELLWOOD, Jr., is Bishop James W. Bashford Professor of Oriental Studies in the School of Religion of the University of Southern California, Los Angeles. He received his BA from the University of Colorado in 1954 and his PhD in history of religions from the University of Chicago in 1967. Besides those works listed in the bibliography of this article, his books include *Many Peoples, Many Faiths*; *Introducing Religion from Inside and Outside*; and *Mysticism and Religion*.

BERT HARDIN, born in 1939, obtained his MA in 1969 with a thesis on 'Community Development and Sociology' and his PhD in 1975. He is at present on the staff of the department of sociology at the University of Tübingen. Among his recent publications on new religious movements are: (with Günther Kehrer) 'Identity and Commitment' in *Identity and Religion* ed. Hans Mol (1978); 'Rückzug in die Innerlichkeit? Jugendsekten als moralisches Alternativerlebnis' in *Gefährdete Jugend* ed. Martin Furian (1980); (with Günther Kehrer) 'Enstehung und Entwicklung der Vereinigungskirche in der Bundesrepublik Deutschland' in *Das Entstehen einer neuen Religion* ed. Günther Kehrer (1981); (with Günter Kehrer) 'Some Social Factors affecting the Rejection of New Belief Systems' in *New Religious Movements: A Perspective for Understanding Society* ed. Eileen Barker (1982); 'Aspekte des Phänomens neuer religiöser Bewegungen in der Bundesrepublik Deutschland', due to appear in *Social Compass*, 1 (1983).

REINHART HUMMEL, who was born in 1930, worked as a pastor in Schleswig-Holstein after studying theology and gaining his degree in New Testament studies. From 1966 to 1973 he was principal of a theological college at Kotapad, India, and then became a research assistant at Heidelberg. In 1979 he gained his *Habilitation* in the field of religion and missiology. Since 1981 he has been head of the Protestant Centre for Questions of Religious Belief and Outlook. Among his publications are: *Indische Mission und neue Frömmigkeit im Westen* (Stuttgart 1980); 'Weltverbesserung und Idealgesellschaft. Zum Verständnis indischer Meditationsbewegungen im Westen' in

Zeitschrift für Religions- und Geistesgeschichte 30 (1978) 129-152; 'Hinduistische Gurus und Gruppen im Westen' in *Reformatio* 28 (1979) 165-178; 'Jugendreligionen—missionierende Gemeinschaften?' in *Zeitschrift für Mission* (1981) pp. 135-140.

CHRISTOPHER O DONNELL, OCarm, was born in 1936 in Dublin, Ireland. He is a Carmelite and was ordained in 1963. He studied at University College and Milltown Institute in Dublin and at the Gregorian University, Rome. He lectures in systematic theology at the Milltown Pontifical Institute of Theology and Philosophy. He has been involved in charismatic renewal for eight years and has experience of it in Southern Africa as well as the United States and Europe. His publications include *Life in the Spirit and Mary* (Delaware-Dublin 1981), contributions to two volumes of ecumenical studies, *Who are We? What do we Believe* ed. S. Worrall (Belfast 1977), *Church and Eucharist* ed. M. Hurley (Dublin 1966) and to two commentaries on Vatican II, Constitution on the Church ed. A. Flannery (Dublin-Chicago 1966) and ed. K. McNamara (Dublin-Melbourne 1968).

DANIEL J. O'HANLON, SJ, was born in 1919. His graduate work in theology was done at the Gregorian University in Rome and the University of Tübingen, followed by postgraduate work at Syracuse University and the Harvard Divinity School. He was active in the Catholic-Protestant ecumenical dialogue of the 1960s and served on the staff of the Secretariat for Christian Unity in Rome during the Second Vatican Council. During the 1970s he explored at first hand the ways in which the religious traditions of Asia can enrich Christian theology and spiritual practice. Recently he has begun to investigate how the resources of humanistic and transpersonal psychology can be integrated into Christian spiritual practice. He has been visiting professor of religion at Stanford University and at the University of California at Santa Barbara. Since 1958 he has been on the faculty of the Jesuit School of Theology at Berkeley, a member of the Graduate Theological Union which was formerly Alma College at Los Gatos, California.

Recent writings include 'Zen and the Spiritual Exercises' in *Theological Studies* 39, No. 4 (December 1978); 'Truth Power (Nonviolence): the Central Theme of Thomas Merton' in *Spirituality Today* 32, No. 2 (June 1980) (reprinted in *Catholic Mind* 79, No. 1354 (June 1981)); and 'Integration of Spiritual Practices: A Western Christian looks East' in *Journal of Transpersonal Theology* 13, No. 2 (1981).

THOMAS ROBBINS is a sociologist in religion. He is in the sociology department at Central Michigan University in Mt Pleasant, Michigan. He has co-edited (with Dick Anthony) *In Gods We Trust: New Patterns of Religious Pluralism in America* (Transaction 1981) and (with Dick Anthony and Jacob Needleman) 'Conversion, Coercion and Commitment' in *New Religious Movements* (Crossroads, forthcoming). He is a co-author (with Dick Anthony and Robert Bellah) of a volume dealing with the relationship between religion and social science (in preparation). He has published numerous articles on religious movements, including 'Church, State and Cult' *Sociological Analyst* (Fall, 1981); and 'Deprogramming. Brainwashing and the Medicalization of Deviant Religious Groups' *Social Problems* (February 1982).

PAUL ANTHONY SCHWARTZ is project director of the Center for the Study of New Religious Movements at the Graduate Theological Union in Berkeley, California, where he is a candidate for the PhD in the field of religion and society. He has studied the use of religious testimonials in several new religious groups in Quebec and is currently preparing a volume (with James McBride) on the Moral Majority in the United States.

CONCILIUM

91. **The Church as Institution.** Ed. Gregory Baum and Andrew Greeley. 0 8164 2575 2 168pp.
92. **Politics and Liturgy.** Ed. Herman Schmidt and David Power. 0 8164 2576 0 156pp.
93. **Jesus Christ and Human Freedom.** Ed. Edward Schillebeeckx and Bas van Iersel. 0 8164 2577 9 168pp.
94. **The Experience of Dying.** Ed. Norbert Greinacher and Alois Müller. 0 8164 2578 7 156pp.
95. **Theology of Joy.** Ed. Johannes Baptist Metz and Jean-Pierre Jossua. 0 8164 2579 5 164pp.
96. **The Mystical and Political Dimension of the Christian Faith.** Ed. Claude Geffré and Gustavo Guttierez. 0 8164 2580 9 168pp.
97. **The Future of the Religious Life.** Ed. Peter Huizing and William Bassett. 0 8164 2094 7 96pp.
98. **Christians and Jews.** Ed. Hans Küng and Walter Kasper. 0 8164 2095 5 96pp.
99. **Experience of the Spirit.** Ed. Peter Huizing and William Bassett. 0 8164 2096 3 144pp.
100. **Sexuality in Contemporary Catholicism.** Ed. Franz Bockle and Jacques Marie Pohier. 0 8164 2097 1 144pp.
101. **Ethnicity.** Ed. Andrew Greeley and Gregory Baum. 0 8164 2145 5 120pp.
102. **Liturgy and Cultural Religious Traditions.** Ed. Herman Schmidt and David Power. 0 8164 2146 2 120pp.
103. **A Personal God?** Ed. Edward Schillebeeckx and Bas van Iersel. 0 8164 2149 8 142pp.
104. **The Poor and the Church.** Ed. Norbert Greinacher and Alois Müller. 0 8164 2147 1 128pp.
105. **Christianity and Socialism.** Ed. Johannes Baptist Metz and Jean-Pierre Jossua. 0 8164 2148 X 144pp.
106. **The Churches of Africa: Future Prospects.** Ed. Claude Geffré and Bertrand Luneau. 0 8164 2150 1 128pp.
107. **Judgement in the Church.** Ed. William Bassett and Peter Huizing. 0 8164 2166 8 128pp.
108. **Why Did God Make Me?** Ed. Hans Küng and Jürgen Moltmann. 0 8164 2167 6 112pp.
109. **Charisms in the Church.** Ed. Christian Duquoc and Casiano Floristán. 0 8164 2168 4 128pp.
110. **Moral Formation and Christianity.** Ed. Franz Bockle and Jacques Marie Pohier. 0 8164 2169 2 120pp.
111. **Communication in the Church.** Ed. Gregory Baum and Andrew Greeley. 0 8164 2170 6 126pp.
112. **Liturgy and Human Passage.** Ed. David Power and Luis Maldonado. 0 8164 2608 2 136pp.
113. **Revelation and Experience.** Ed. Edward Schillebeeckx and Bas van Iersel. 0 8164 2609 0 134pp.
114. **Evangelization in the World Today.** Ed. Norbert Greinacher and Alois Müller. 0 8164 2610 4 136pp.

115. **Doing Theology in New Places.** Ed. Jean-Pierre Jossua and Johannes Baptist Metz. 0 8164 2611 2 120pp.
116. **Buddhism and Christianity.** Ed. Claude Geffré and Mariasusai Dhavamony, 0 8164 2612 0 136pp.
117. **The Finances of the Church.** Ed. William Bassett and Peter Huizing. 0 8164 2197 8 160pp.
118. **An Ecumenical Confession of Faith?** Ed. Hans Küng and Jürgen Moltmann. 0 8164 2198 6 136pp.
119. **Discernment of the Spirit and of Spirits.** Ed. Casiano Floristán and Christian Duquoc. 0 8164 2199 4 136pp.
120. **The Death Penalty and Torture.** Ed. Franz Bockle and Jacques Marie Pohier. 0 8164 2200 1 136pp.
121. **The Family in Crisis or in Transition.** Ed. Andrew Greely. 0 567 30001 3 128pp.
122. **Structures of Initiation in Crisis.** Ed. Luis Maldonado and David Power. 0 567 30002 1 128pp.
123. **Heaven.** Ed. Bas van Iersel and Edward Schillebeeckx. 0 567 30003 X 120pp.
124. **The Church and the Rights of Man.** Ed. Alois Müller and Norbert Greinacher. 0 567 30004 8 140pp.
125. **Christianity and the Bourgeoisie.** Ed. Johannes Baptist Metz. 0 567 30005 6 144pp.
126. **China as a Challenge to the Church.** Ed. Claude Geffré and Joseph Spae. 0 567 30006 4 136pp.
127. **The Roman Curia and the Communion of Churches.** Ed. Peter Huizing and Knut Walf. 0 567 30007 2 144pp.
128. **Conflicts about the Holy Spirit.** Ed. Hans Küng and Jürgen Moltmann. 0 567 30008 0 144pp.
129. **Models of Holiness.** Ed. Christian Duquoc and Casiano Floristán. 0 567 30009 9 128pp.
130. **The Dignity of the Despised of the Earth.** Ed. Jacques Marie Pohier and Dietmar Mieth. 0 567 30010 2 144pp.
131. **Work and Religion.** Ed. Gregory Baum. 0 567 30011 0 148pp.
132. **Symbol and Art in Worship.** Ed. Luis Maldonado and David Power. 0 567 30012 9 136pp.
133. **Right of the Community to a Priest.** Ed. Edward Schillebeeckx and Johannes Baptist Metz. 0 567 30013 7 148pp.
134. **Women in a Men's Church.** Ed. Virgil Elizondo and Norbert Greinacher. 0 567 30014 5 144pp.
135. **True and False Universality of Christianity.** Ed. Claude Geffré and Jean-Pierre Jossua. 0 567 30015 3 138pp.
136. **What is Religion? An Inquiry for Christian Theology.** Ed. Mircea Eliade and David Tracy. 0 567 30016 1 98pp.
137. **Electing our Own Bishops.** Ed. Peter Huizing and Knut Walf. 0 567 30017 X 112pp.

138. **Conflicting Ways of Interpreting the Bible.** Ed. Hans Küng and Jürgen Moltmann. 0 567 30018 8 112pp.
139. **Christian Obedience.** Ed. Casiano Floristán and Christian Duquoc. 0 567 30019 6 96pp.
140. **Christian Ethics and Economics: the North-South Conflict.** Ed. Dietmar Mieth and Jacques Marie Pohier. 0 567 30020 X 128pp.
141. **Neo-Conservatism: Social and Religious Phenomenon.** Ed. Gregory Baum and John Coleman. 0 567 30021 8.
142. **The Times of Celebration.** Ed. David Power and Mary Collins. 0 567 30022 6.
143. **God as Father.** Ed. Edward Schillebeeckx and Johannes Baptist Metz. 0 567 30023 4.
144. **Tensions Between the Churches of the First World and the Third World.** Ed. Virgil Elizondo and Norbert Greinacher. 0 567 30024 2.
145. **Nietzsche and Christianity.** Ed. Claude Geffré and Jean-Pierre Jossua. 0 567 30025 0.
146. **Where Does the Church Stand?** Ed. Giuseppe Alberigo. 0 567 30026 9.
147. **The Revised Code of Canon Law: a Missed Opportunity?** Ed. Peter Huizing and Knut Walf. 0 567 30027 7.
148. **Who Has the Say in the Church?** Ed. Hans Küng and Jürgen Moltmann. 0 567 30028 5.
149. **Francis of Assisi Today.** Ed. Casiano Floristán and Christian Duquoc. 0 567 30029 3.
150. **Christian Ethics: Uniformity, Universality, Pluralism.** Ed. Jacques Pohier and Dietmar Mieth. 0 567 30030 7.
151. **The Church and Racism.** Ed. Gregory Baum and John Coleman. 0 567 30031 5.
152. **Can we always celebrate the Eucharist?** Ed. Mary Collins and David Power. 0 567 30032 3.
153. **Jesus, Son of God?** Ed. Edward Schillebeeckx and Johannes-Baptist Metz. 0 567 30033 1.
154. **Religion and Churches in Eastern Europe.** Ed. Virgil Elizondo and Norbert Greinacher. 0 567 30034 X.
155. **'The Human', Criterion of Christian Existence?** Ed. Claude Geffré and Jean-Pierre Jossua. 0 567 30035 8.
156. **The Challenge of Psychology to Faith.** Ed. Steven Kepnes (Guest Editor) and David Tracy. 0 567 30036 6.
157. **May Church Ministers be Politicians?** Ed. Peter Huizing and Knut Walf. 0 567 30037 4.
158. **The Right to Dissent.** Ed. Hans Küng and Jürgen Moltmann. 0 567 30038 2.
159. **Learning to Pray.** Ed. Casiano Floristán and Christian Duquoc. 0 567 30039 0.
160. **Unemployment and the Right to Work.** Ed. Dietmar Mieth and Jacques Pohier. 0 567 30040 4.

All back issues are still in print and available for sale. Orders should be sent to the publishers,

T. & T. CLARK LIMITED

▬ 36 George Street, Edinburgh EH2 2LQ, Scotland ▬